NATURE BY DESIGN

NATURE BY DESIGN

THE PRACTICE OF BIOPHILIC DESIGN

STEPHEN R. KELLERT

Yale UNIVERSITY PRESS/NEW HAVEN & LONDON

We gratefully acknowledge funding from Interface, Inc.,
which supported the research and illustrations program.

Frontispiece: The Portcullis House courtyard, designed by Hopkins
Architects Partnership LLP, connects parliamentary offices in London. It is a
compelling and enthralling combination of both direct and indirect biophilic
design features. The natural world is brought inside by the column of trees
and the water pools. And the spiderweb-like framing of the roof and its
skylights makes the connection to nature even more dramatic.

Yale University Press books may be purchased in quantity for educational,
business, or promotional use. For information, please e-mail
sales.press@yale.edu (U.S. office) or sales@yaleup.co.uk (U.K. office).

Designed by Mary Valencia.
Set in Adobe Garamond type by Tseng Information Systems, Inc.
Printed in China.

Library of Congress Control Number: 2017943458
ISBN 978-0-300-21453-6 (hardcover : alk. paper)

A catalogue record for this book is available from the British Library.

This paper meets the requirements of ANSI/NISO Z39.48-1992
(Permanence of Paper).

10 9 8 7 6 5 4 3 2 1

CONTENTS

PREFACE

*B*iophilia refers to the inherent affinity people have for the natural world. This inborn tendency developed during the long course of human evolution when people largely adapted to natural, not artificial or human-made, forces. Assuming this biological inclination continues to be vital to human health and wellbeing, one of the great challenges of our time is to foster beneficial contact with nature in our built environments, where we now on average spend 90 percent of our time. The challenge of biophilic design—biophilia in the human-built environment—is the focus of this book.

People have, in fact, practiced forms of biophilic design over the ages, although largely in an intuitive and iterative manner, influenced by factors related to history, geography, ecology, and culture. Today we are compelled to take a more systematic and deliberate approach to the application of biophilic design, for two reasons. First, our society has largely assumed an adversarial relationship to nature, mainly seeing it as an obstacle to dominate and overcome—a mere natural resource to be transformed through technology to some higher use, or a nice, but not necessary, recreational and aesthetic amenity. Stressing the importance of nature in our largely constructed and created world is often viewed as a low priority and romantic perspective. To advance the objectives of biophilic design, we must demonstrate that nature substantially enhances human physical and mental health, performance, and wellbeing. Second, the rapid pace and large-scale approach of much modern development has magnified the adverse effects of ignoring the need for biophilic design and made these effects difficult to correct. We can no longer rely on good intentions and architectural insight to effectively incorporate nature into the built environment. Biophilic design provides instead a more deliberate, systematic, and informed approach to bringing beneficial contact with nature into the modern built environment.

This book offers a rationale, framework, and methodology for accomplishing this objective. Yet it is far from the final word on the subject. The understanding of biophilic design has been rapidly evolving in recent years and is still a relatively new approach. Additional improvements will undoubtedly occur as a result of new knowledge and refinements in the years ahead.

A number of important biophilic design publications and online manuscripts have appeared in recent years that have greatly assisted the author in writing this book. Of special importance have been initiatives of the design studio Terrapin Bright Green, particularly the work of Bill Browning and Catie Ryan on "14 Patterns of Biophilic Design and the Economics of Biophilia." In addition, the insightful and prolific biophilic design work of Judith Heerwagen, an environmental psychologist at the University of Washington, has been exceptionally helpful. The work of the architect Nikos Salingaros and the Living Building Challenge have further provided important understandings, insights, and methodologies.

This book will inevitably reflect my biases and limitations. Moreover, my aim is not to specify how biophilic design should be applied in every circumstance. Variations in setting, cost, and culture will inevitably result in a wide diversity of applications of biophilic design. To paraphrase Judith Heerwagen, biophilic design does not tell a designer or developer what he or she should do, but rather what is important. Once the significance of biophilic design has been established and ways suggested for how it may occur, a wide choice of possibilities emerge for effectively incorporating nature into the built environment. What this book does do is present basic principles, practices, and strategies for achieving biophilic design. The goal is to identify a menu of options, which the designer can then employ depending on a project's particular conditions and circumstances.

A basic consideration is how biophilic design relates to what has been called sustainability or low-environmental-impact design. As the term implies, low-environmental-impact design is intended to minimize and avoid the adverse effects of the built environment on natural systems and human health that result from such practices as excess resource and energy use, pollution, climate emissions, loss of biodiversity, and more. Biophilic design embodies the opposite side of the same coin—how human health and wellbeing can be enriched through beneficial contact with natural systems and processes. True and lasting sustainability depends on combining low-environmental-impact and biophilic design. Low-environmental-impact design aims to minimize the damaging effects of the built environment, whereas biophilic design provides the rationale and motivation to maintain and be good stewards of our buildings, landscapes, and communities. If only one approach to sustainability is used, the resulting creation tends to fail both people and nature over time.

Because I am a scientifically trained scholar, my other books have mostly relied on the written word and statistics to convey knowledge and advocate certain policy positions. Having worked with designers and developers over the past several years, however, I have come to appreciate the important roles of graphic designers and illustrators. For example, I recall when an architect friend who read an earlier book of mine on biophilic design, and then saw a film we made of the subject, turned to me following the video and said: "Steve, now I get it. I'm an architect. I need to see pictures before I understand anything." To those professionals for whom an illustration may be worth a thousand words, this book provides some relief in employing more than one hundred figures, though even this large number hardly measures up to the complexity and importance of its message.

Selecting these illustrations was a time-consuming and often difficult challenge, and securing permission for their use sometimes even more so. For making this process immeasurably more feasible, I want to thank Melissa Flamson and her colleagues at the company With Permission. In addition, the graphic artists Stephen Harrington and Bill Nelson provided a number of highly effective and evocative line illustrations.

Including so many color illustrations in a larger format book could not have occurred without the invaluable support of the Interface, Inc. I especially appreciate the assistance and support of David Gerson in this regard. Interface, founded by the visionary Ray Anderson, has long championed and pioneered the practice of sustainability and biophilic design.

Once again, I deeply appreciate the support, advice, and encouragement of my extraordinary senior executive editor at Yale University Press, Jean Thomson Black, and her assistant, Michael Deneen. I also greatly appreciate all the support provided by my wife, Cilla.

ONE

BIOPHILIA

THE NATURE OF HUMAN NATURE

We live in a remarkable age previously beyond imagination. In today's world, we have access to vast amounts of information practically at our fingertips, as well as a wide array of products and materials. We also possess the ability to communicate across enormous distances in a matter of seconds, an average life span of eighty years, and the power to construct in a few years buildings and even cities that once took decades or sometimes centuries to build. By contrast, for more than 99 percent of our species' history the average human life was short, uncertain, brutish, and preoccupied with a daily struggle against famine, disease, and painful death. People largely depended on local resources and rarely ventured far from where they were born.

In effect, for much of human history, people's everyday lives were closely aligned with nature. Consequently, the human body, mind, and spirit largely developed in adaptive response to mainly environmental forces. In this world, people depended on responding quickly to threats and opportunities associated with the natural world. Knowledge of plants, animals, soils, water, landscapes, and an array of ecological cues (for example, color, shape, form, light, weather, information richness, organized complexity, prospect, and opportunities for refuge) largely determined whether people would survive, reproduce, and thrive.

Although most creatures mainly relied on speed, strength, stealth, prowess, and other physical powers, humans primarily employed the brain and its capacities for reasoning, intelligence, and symbolic thought in order to ensure their safety, sustenance, and security. This remarkable mental prowess allowed people to reach beyond their physical limitations and eventually to use their imaginations for creative, inventive endeavors. Cognitive capacity allowed our species to flourish and become increasingly capable of exploiting and controlling the natural world. In time, we achieved a kind of mastery over nature, subduing and transforming the natural world through critical thinking, problem solving, and technological innovation.

Yet fear and the need to protect ourselves from nature still ruled much of our lives. Moreover, and just as functionally, so did our aesthetic attraction and emotional attachment to certain elements of our natural environment, which even today are reflected in our capacities to experience beauty and affection in nature, and ultimately, to sense an underlying order in the world. All this facilitated our ability to symbolize nature, projecting its image and understanding in the process of developing our capacity for communication, language, and culture.

In these and other ways, humans evolved in close association with the natural world. In time, humans' successful adaptations to nature became biologically encoded, resulting in a diverse set of inclinations to affiliate with natural patterns and processes. This inherent tendency to interact with and experience nature has been called biophilia. Of great importance and lingering uncertainty, however, is whether or not biophilia remains adaptive in modern society, or instead has become largely obsolete and vestigial—once relevant in circumstances where it originally developed, but no longer of meaningful significance in contemporary society.

Complicating this uncertainty further, the inclination to affiliate with nature, like much of what makes us human, is not a hard-wired instinctual response that occurs among all people and with the slightest provocation. Instead, biophilia relies on experience, learning, and social support to develop and become functionally beneficial. Unfor-

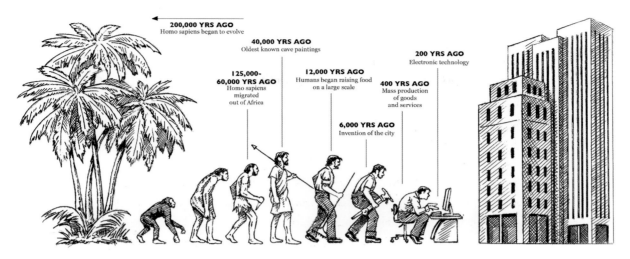

Figure 1.1. For much of human history, people evolved in adaptive response to natural, not human-made, forces and stimuli. This figure provides a somewhat facetious perspective of the human shift from living mainly in nature to surviving in today's designed and built world. Ancient cave and modern electronic humans amusingly resemble one another in their inclination to bend rather than stand erect.

tunately, modern society has increasingly viewed the experience of nature as a mere vestige of the past, a remnant now largely reflected in a dispensable recreational and aesthetic amenity. People are ever more separated from nature in today's world, especially in the modern city and built environment.

This growing disconnect from nature is due to many factors. Fundamentally, it reflects the underlying assumptions of a technologically oriented, sedentary society that spends most of its time indoors and regards exposure to nature as mainly primitive and backward. Figure 1.1 depicts one facetious view of the continuing evolutionary significance of humans in the modern world.

Despite our temptation to dismiss the importance of nature, mounting evidence suggests that our inborn tendency to connect with the natural world continues to be highly important for human health, productivity, and wellbeing. From this perspective, a major challenge of our time is determining how to incorporate the beneficial experience of nature into the built environment. The objective of those who care about biophilic design is to create good habitat for people as biological animals in the places we live, work, and reside.

Because this book focuses on satisfying the conditions of biophilia in the built environment, the temptation is to move quickly to this focus on biophilic design. This would be a mistake, however, given that many observed failures and shortcomings of biophilic design have reflected an insufficient understanding of biophilia. Biophilic design does not involve simply applying any form of nature to the built environment, but rather doing so in ways that effectively satisfy the inherent human inclination to affiliate with the natural world. As E. O. Wilson (1984) so poetically explains, biophilia is "the innate tendency to focus on life and lifelike processes . . . To affiliate with life is a deep and complicated process in mental development. To an extent still undervalued in philosophy and religion, our existence depends on this propensity, our spirit is woven from it, hope rises on its currents" (p. 1).

The concept of biophilia refers to aspects of nature that have figured most prominently in human evolution and development. This may appear to be a straightforward notion, but on closer examination it is a complex consideration. It leaves unanswered the question of which aspects of nature have been especially critical in advancing human health and wellbeing. It also fails to cite the ways in which people are inherently inclined to attach meaning to, derive benefit from, and, in effect, value the natural world. Finally, it avoids the question of how people can internalize or learn from their experience of nature to the extent that it actually enhances their health, productivity, and wellbeing. I provide a detailed examination of these issues in my 2012 book *Birthright: People and Nature in the Modern World*. Still, these issues should be briefly addressed here, and serve as the basis for the basic principles and practices of biophilic design described in subsequent chapters.

The human biological response to nature has tended to focus on certain species and natural processes that have figured most prominently in human evolution and development. For example, people are especially prone to react to other forms of life that have been particularly connected with our survival: consider those creatures that facilitated our sustenance and safety, such as horses, dogs, and cattle; large and fearsome predators like wolves, great cats, and bears; and a wide variety of other species (estimated at nearly a hundred thousand) that have significantly affected human success. We are also predisposed to like certain edible, flowering, and fruiting plants, as well as to avoid those that are typically regarded as potentially toxic or dangerous. Other natural conditions of special significance to people have included qualities of light and air, the availability and drinkability of water, the vagaries of weather, and a host of ecological characteristics, knowledge of which advanced human security and wellbeing. For example, certain landscapes and geological forms have been found to be especially important in human evolution, such as savannah-type settings, forested edges, watercourses, mountains, and valleys.

Without question, certain senses have been especially critical for human evolution and survival. Humans are primarily and historically diurnal or daytime creatures, and as a result, vision is especially important and dominant. Those who could see long distances, use color to spot resources and opportunities, and visually organize and order complex settings fared better and so had an evolutionary advantage. Humans further developed the ability to respond quickly to natural settings by using a variety of strategies such as utilizing prospect and refuge (gaining a clear view of the landscape from a safe and secure spot), employing certain natural geometries, processing the information richness of nature, and developing ecological and human social connections to place.

All these and more have all emerged as relevant to the practice of biophilic design, because these various preferential responses to nature determine how people can feel more comfortable, satisfied, secure, healthy, and productive in their built environments. Consequently, it is not enough to include just one natural feature or attribute in such spaces. Instead the effective practice of biophilic design depends on knowing and appreciating which features and processes of the natural world have been especially relevant to human functioning and so will offer the greatest benefit to people in today's modern setting.

Toward this end, eight values of biophilia have been identified, each potentially relevant to the advancement of human health and fitness, and each a legitimate focus and outcome of biophilic design (Kellert 2012). The content and priority of these values vary greatly depending on people's distinctive backgrounds, experience, learning, and cultures. Yet each value is universally present in all humans, contributing in different ways to human welfare and wellbeing.

The eight biophilic values and their frequently associated benefits are

· *Affection:* The human tendency to express strong emotional attachment and at times love for features of the natural world. Commonly associated benefits include the ability to bond, care, and connect emotionally with others.

· *Attraction:* People's inherent aesthetic attraction and ability to perceive beauty in nature. Associated benefits include feelings of harmony and symmetry, emotional and intellectual development, and enhanced capacities for imagination and creativity.

· *Aversion:* The inclination to avoid aspects of nature that generate feelings of anxiety, threat, and sometimes fear. Benefits include enhanced safety and security, coping and competitive skills, and sometimes a sense of awe and respect for powers greater than one's own.

· *Control:* The tendency to master, dominate, and, at times, subjugate nature. Benefits include enhanced mastery and problem-solving skills, critical thinking, and cognitive development.

· *Exploitation:* The tendency to utilize the natural world as a source of materials and resources. Commonly associated benefits include enhanced security, extractive abilities, and practical skills.

· *Intellect:* The inclination to use nature as a means for advancing rational thought and intellectual development. Benefits include cognitive skills, empirical and observational abilities, critical thinking, and learning.

· *Symbolism:* The tendency to employ the image of nature to advance communication and abstract thought. Important benefits include the capacities for language and culture, intellectual development, and enhanced imagination and creativity.

· *Spirituality:* The inclination to experience nature as a means for achieving a sense of meaning, purpose, and connection to creation. Associated benefits include feelings of meaningful and purposeful existence, enhanced self-confidence, and bonding with others.

The adaptive occurrence of any biophilic value depends on experience, learning, and social support. People do not benefit from contact with nature unless this involves engaging and recurring, rather than isolated, experiences. Effectively incorporating nature into people's lives in a lasting, meaningful way requires building a supportive learning environment that relates to people's everyday world, and encouraging the involvement of significant others such as family, friends, peers, and community members. Single or sporadic exposures to nature that have only limited relevance to others typically exert little lasting benefit over time.

The importance of these values of biophilia and their dependence on learning and experience raises the question: what does biophilia have to do with the design of the modern built environment? Although we will delve into this subject more fully in Chapter 2, a few points are worth stressing here.

First, it should be evident that not all experiences of nature are necessarily biophilic; some can be quite trivial and insignificant. Building and landscape designs that have incorporated meaningful contact with nature speak to those evolved tendencies to affiliate with the natural world that have proven instrumental to human health and wellbeing over time, rather than those exposures to nature that have had little lasting significance.

Second, each biophilic value represents an inherent tendency to affiliate with nature that can potentially contribute to human health, performance, and wellbeing, thus each value is a worthy objective of biophilic design. The exploitation and control of nature, for instance, are no more intrinsically important to the design of the built environment than is protection from elements that provoke anxiety or the fostering of an emotional attachment or aesthetic attraction to the natural world. Moreover, most of our most successful building and landscape designs often respond to a wide range of biophilic values. Of course, certain structures tend to emphasize certain biophilic values over others—a manufacturing complex is likely to stress the exploitation of nature, an educational facility learning and cognitive development, and a house of worship spiritual growth and commitment. Yet the more biophilic values a particular building or landscape embodies, regardless of its particular use, the more likely its design will generate numerous benefits—and motivate people to cherish and sustain these structures over time.

Finally, biophilia's reliance on learning and development to become functionally beneficial means that successful biophilic design depends on engaging, immersive, and ecologically connected experiences of nature. People must be part of a reinforcing and coherent environment. It is no accident that some of the most unsuccessful attempts at bringing nature into the built environment involve only isolated and sporadic exposures rather than repeated, engaging, and interconnected contact with natural features and processes.

IS BIOPHILIA STILL RELEVANT?

Skepticism about biophilia and biophilic design reflects doubts about its continuing relevance in modern society. Some view biophilia as obsolete, a remnant of the time when human survival depended on close association with and knowledge of the natural world. This possibility may be countered by the findings of a study that exposed subjects to subliminal images (15 to 30 milliseconds) of snakes, spiders, handguns, and frayed electric wires. The great majority of study participants responded aversively to the subliminal images of snakes and spiders, while remaining unresponsive to the far more contemporary threats of handguns and exposed wires (Öhman 1986).

A growing body of research is proving that exposure to nature can exert a significant impact on people's physical and mental health, performance, and wellbeing. These studies have occurred in a wide diversity of settings, including hospitals, workplaces, schools, recreational facilities, and neighborhood communities. Most of this research is methodologically limited, involving small and nonrandomly selected samples, a lack of controls, very little experimental or even quasi-experimental research, limited data collection, poorly validated measures, and at times biased interpretation of results. Still, they collectively provide a compelling picture of the continuing importance of exposure to nature for human wellness—even as some wonder whether the very need for scientific proof may reflect a society so alienated from its biological roots that it may be the first in human history to demand evidence that nature is good for people.

For example, various healthcare studies have reported that exposure to nature can reduce stress, lower blood pressure, provide pain relief, and contribute to healing and recovery from illness. Among hospital staff, contact with nature has been linked to employee satisfaction and morale, improved performance, and enhanced recruitment and retention. A 2011 review of more than one hundred healthcare studies (Annerstedt and Währborg 2011) reported a wide spectrum of physical, mental, and behavioral benefits associated with exposure to nature.

In another example, Roger Ulrich (1984) undertook a study of patients recovering from gallbladder surgery who were demographically similar and randomly assigned to hospital rooms. All rooms had windows, although some offered a view of a brick wall, whereas others overlooked an ordinary tree grove. The patients assigned to the rooms with the brick wall view had slower recovery times, required more potent painkillers, expressed greater dissatisfaction with their care, and generated more frequent complaints according to nursing notes. By contrast, Ulrich reported, "Patients with the nature window view had shorter post-surgical hospital stays ... fewer minor post-surgical complications, far fewer negative comments in nurses' notes. The wall view patients required far more potent pain killers" (107).

Positive health benefits have also been reported among disabled and sick children exposed to nature. These studies indicate higher rates of adult diabetes, myopia, and obesity among children lacking contact with nature, while exposure to nature is correlated with reductions in allergies, asthma, and, at times, symptoms of autism and attention deficit disorder.

Various work-related studies have reported physical and mental improvements associated with increased exposure to nature. These benefits include enhanced health, improved morale and motivation, better worker performance, and superior employee recruitment and retention. Research focusing on office workers found that improvements in natural lighting, exposure to plants, outside views, and pictures of nature often contributed to employee performance and wellbeing. A largely anecdotal study reported that better natural lighting, the design of interior park-like spaces, and water features led to highly paid professionals volunteering to work longer hours and collaborating more. Yet the average office worker in the United States toils in a windowless and largely sensory-deprived environment. These often-featureless settings have been compared to the barren cages of an old-style zoo, the kinds of enclosures that are now, ironically, banned as inhumane for nonhuman animals.

Judith Heerwagen (2000) has conducted perhaps the most significant work-related research in biophilic design to date. The office and manufacturing complex she studied, designed for an office-furniture manufacturer by the architect William McDonough, includes such biophilic features as extensive interior vegetation, widespread natural lighting, a restored prairie landscape, trails, and sitting places. Surveys administered to workers before, immediately after, and nine months following the project's completion found, even after nine months, a 22 percent increase in worker productivity, significant gains in worker motivation and emotional satisfaction, reductions in absenteeism and stress, and a 20 percent increase in a "sense of well-being."

Conventionally designed schools typically emphasize indoor, nonexperiential, abstract learning that removes students from contact with nature. Some schools, however, have incorporated natural lighting, natural materials, interior plants, and exposure to the outside environment. Studies have generally found that students in these schools have higher test scores, as well as improved attendance and motivation; teachers and other staff, too, have better performance, morale, recruitment, and retention. A recent national study (Kellert and David J. Case & Associates 2016) of some 1,500 eight- to twelve-year-old children and their parents found that increasing the children's contact with nature correlated with superior learning and development. Children with greater exposure to nature reported greater physical strength and coordination, better self-esteem and self-confidence, an enhanced ability to cope with challenge and adversity, and higher critical-thinking, problem-solving, and creative abilities.

At the community and urban scales, research findings have indicated that the presence of trees, open space, and other appealing natural features often can contribute to resident health and wellbeing. One study of a 250-square-mile watershed in south-central Connecticut examined the relationship among environmental quality, human quality of life, and environmental values among eighteen rural, suburban, and urban neighborhoods. Such environmental quality indicators as pollution levels, amount of nonindigenous plants, hydrological flow, and nutrient flux were significantly correlated to the residents' quality of life. This relationship applied to all socioeconomic groups and occurred in urban as well as nonurban communities.

The universality of this finding is important because many dismiss contact with nature as a luxury for those with the time and resources to enjoy it, and so as an experience largely irrelevant to impoverished people who have more immediate practical priorities. Yet research at a Chicago public housing project among very poor residents revealed a strong correlation between exposure to nature and various physical and mental health benefits. The public housing project consisted of architecturally unattractive high-rise buildings, some surrounded by poorly maintained grass and trees, and others, by concrete and asphalt. After controlling for many potentially confounding factors, the researchers reported that those living in housing units surrounded by vegetation had superior coping abilities, greater optimism, lower drug and crime rates, a greater knowledge of their neighbors, and better cognitive functioning than those living in buildings surrounded by only a hard, unnatural surface.

Kathleen Wolf and colleagues (2015) at the University of Washington, in collaboration with the U.S. Forest Service, have summarized the health and social benefits of

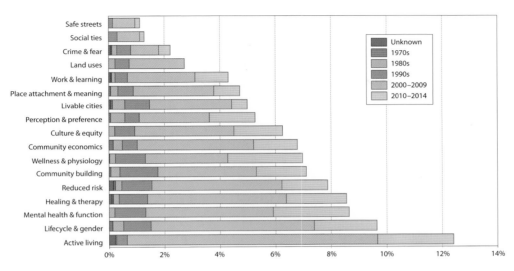

Figure 1.2. Frequency of various characteristics of urban life, from the article database for Green Cities: Good Health, a web portal to scientific evidence concerning the relationships of metro nature to human health and wellness. The article database contains about 3,100 peer-reviewed journal articles and reports, as well as technical reports from agencies, universities, and non-governmental organizations. The website, www.green health.washington.edu, is sponsored by the University of Washington, and the project director is Kathleen L. Wolf, Ph.D. Funding for assembling the database and preparing the literature summaries is provided by the USDA Forest Service.

people living in urban environments with greater contact with nature. They drew on a database of more than three thousand peer-reviewed studies, sourced from nations all around the world. Although these research projects are often substantially different from one another, they consistently indicate that exposure to nature in urban areas contributes important physical and mental health gains and community-level improvements (Figure 1.2).

This limited review of studies in health, work, education, childhood development, and urban planning supports the conclusion that biophilia, instead of being irrelevant and vestigial, continues to play a critical role in the relation of nature to human health and wellbeing. Even in our increasingly urban society, exposure to natural features and processes remains an anvil on which human fitness and wellbeing are forged. Denying or diminishing this need for contact with nature will likely impoverish the human body, mind, and spirit.

THE MODERN DISCONNECT FROM NATURE

Contemporary society's growing separation from nature, particularly in the design and development of the modern built environment, is partly a function of our increasingly indoor, urban, and technological-oriented existence. It reflects a deeply held belief that progress and civilization depend on the ever-expanding capacity to control, convert, and transcend nature. This conviction is widely encountered in our practices of agriculture, medicine, manufacturing, education, work, urban planning, and design practices related to architecture and other built environments. Modern society typically views nature as mainly an obstacle to overcome through science and technology, or only marginally relevant and so a dispensable aesthetic and recreational amenity.

The prevailing paradigm of modern building and landscape design reflects these assumptions of the limited importance and relevance of contact with nature. The great majority of our structures used for purposes related to healthcare; education; manufacturing; hospitality; commercial, retail, and office tasks; and even religion and spirituality reveal this attitude. These modern constructions are often dominated by the use of human-made materials, artificial lighting, processed air, and sensory-deprived environments with little connection to the culture or ecology of the places where they occur. These structures generally endorse a standard of global "international architecture," where building design

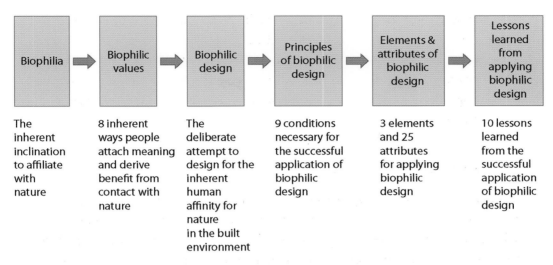

Biophilia	Biophilic values	Biophilic design	Principles of biophilic design	Elements & attributes of biophilic design	Lessons learned from applying biophilic design
The inherent inclination to affiliate with nature	8 inherent ways people attach meaning and derive benefit from contact with nature	The deliberate attempt to design for the inherent human affinity for nature in the built environment	9 conditions necessary for the successful application of biophilic design	3 elements and 25 attributes for applying biophilic design	10 lessons learned from the successful application of biophilic design

Figure 1.3. How does biophilia relate to biophilic design?

and construction are pretty much the same no matter the location of the building or the background, values, or culture of the people involved. As the writer John Le Carré sourly remarked, such structures represent "another chunk of modern nowhere" (Le Carré 2015).

Another indicator of how separated our society has become from the ordinary everyday experience of nature is that the average person today spends an estimated 90 percent of his or her time indoors, with 80 percent of the most economically advanced nations' population residing in an urban area. Many people today, especially contemporary youth, are engaged with electronic media, on average spending more than forty hours a week mainly with computers, cell phones, and television, with less than ten hours on average spent outside. These trends do not prevent a beneficial connection to nature. Meaningful and beneficial exposure to nature can occur in a city, and even in an indoor setting. The prevailing paradigm of design of the modern built environment theoretically could be a major part of the effort to reconnect people beneficially with nature. Buildings and landscapes can be designed that foster and enhance rather than impede beneficial exposure to nature. We designed ourselves into this adversarial and increasingly separated experience of nature, and, theoretically, we can design ourselves out of it. But doing so will require a new paradigm of design for our built environments, one that involves a massive commitment to the practice and implementation of biophilic principles. As Figure 1.3 illustrates, this book will connect the theory of biophilia to the practice of biophilic design through explanations of cutting-edge research as well as historical and modern examples.

PRINCIPLES OF BIOPHILIC DESIGN

One of the great challenges of our time is to bring the beneficial experience of nature into the design of contemporary buildings, landscapes, communities, and cities. Devising strategies for including the natural experience in these built structures requires engaging all of the broad tenets and principles of biophilic design.

Biophilic design can be defined as biophilia applied to the design and development of the human built environment. Biophilic design thus derives from a basic understanding of human evolutionary biology and how our inherent inclination to affiliate with nature has historically contributed and even today continues to contribute to human health, fitness, and wellbeing. The fundamental goal of biophilic design is to create good habitats for people as biological animals. Like all species, human functioning depends on being part of an ecological system of interrelated, mutually reinforcing, and integrated parts that constitute a whole greater than its constituent elements. This means designing the built environment to meet our inherent tendencies to affiliate with nature in ecologically connected and complementary ways.

A number of basic principles of biophilic design emerge from this understanding, each of which constitutes a basic condition for its successful application. Rather than simply inserting nature into the built environment, these principles of biophilic design reflect the understanding that humans evolved in adaptive response to nature, and this knowledge can be used to design buildings and landscapes that advance people's health and productivity. Ineffective applications of nature in the built environment occur when these basic tenets of biophilia are ignored.

These nine universal principles sometimes overlap, and their order of presentation does not suggest any priority of importance. Still, each principle provides a foundation for the effective practice and application of biophilic design.

1. BIOPHILIC DESIGN FOCUSES ON HUMAN ADAPTATIONS TO NATURE THAT ADVANCE PHYSICAL AND MENTAL HEALTH, PERFORMANCE, AND WELLBEING.

Exposure to nature in the built environment should advance human health and productivity. Biophilic design is not effective if it results in little or no sustained impact on people's physical or mental wellbeing. Isolated contact with nature in a building or landscape—a single plant, a sequestered image of nature, an inaccessible green roof—typically yields little beneficial effect over time; instead these elements often become ignored or relegated to a mere decorative object.

2. BIOPHILIC DESIGN CREATES INTERRELATED AND INTEGRATED SETTINGS WHERE THE ECOLOGICAL WHOLE IS EXPERIENCED MORE THAN ITS INDIVIDUAL PARTS.

Biophilic design should create complementary and integrated connections among the constituent parts of an overall setting that together constitute a functioning ecological whole. When contact with nature in the built environment lacks relationships to other experiences of the natural world and the overall design of a space, these occurrences of nature have a limited impact, becoming simply superficial or decorative curiosities. For example, few sustained or substantial benefits arise from a largely inaccessible outdoors area, a skillful but isolated landscape painting, or a vertical green wall at variance with other features of an overall space. These isolated experiences of nature can even at times yield perverse effects, such as reinforcing the human tendency to exploit and subjugate nature for mainly superficial entertainment and aesthetic purposes. Biophilic design should create an overall ecological setting where various forms of relationship to the natural world complement one another and connect with other design features of a space.

3. BIOPHILIC DESIGN ENCOURAGES ENGAGEMENT AND IMMERSION IN NATURAL FEATURES AND PROCESSES.

A built environment that is responsive to human biophilic needs uses engaging and repeated experiences, learning, and social support to become an integral and beneficial part of people's lives. Infrequent and intermittent contact with nature, or nature-based experiences that are largely unsupported by the values and culture of a group, generally result in few long-term benefits. The beneficial experience of natural features and processes necessitates engaging, immersive, and repeated contact that becomes integral to a person's ongoing reality.

4. BIOPHILIC DESIGN IS STRENGTHENED BY SATISFYING A WIDE RANGE OF VALUES THAT PEOPLE INHERENTLY HOLD ABOUT THE NATURAL WORLD.

Chapter 1 described eight inherent ways that people attach meaning to, derive benefit from, and value the natural world. These biophilic values range from the tendency to exploit, control, avoid, and symbolize nature, to expressions of affection, attraction, intellectual interest, and reverence for natural environments. Successful biophilic design satisfies a diversity of these inherent values of nature. Buildings and landscapes that focus on a single value—such as an organically shaped structure that is designed mainly to make an aesthetic statement, a building that is solely intended to exploit nature, or a learning institution that only focuses on cognitive development—generally elicit little long-term attachment, interest, or benefit.

5. SUCCESSFUL BIOPHILIC DESIGN RESULTS IN EMOTIONAL ATTACHMENTS TO STRUCTURES, LANDSCAPES, AND PLACES.

People develop emotional attachments to the spaces they occupy when these places consistently contribute to their comfort, satisfaction, health, productivity, and wellbeing. These spaces become part of their identity, motivating them to become good stewards and sustain these structures. By contrast, when people lack an emotional attachment to particular buildings and places, they typically neglect or even abuse these spaces. Even settings with features that are environmentally friendly, such as energy or resource efficiency and nonpolluting emissions, are rarely well maintained and sustained over time if people's relationships to these structures lack sufficient levels of emotional affection and commitment.

6. BIOPHILIC DESIGN FOSTERS FEELINGS OF MEMBERSHIP IN A COMMUNITY THAT INCLUDES BOTH PEOPLE AND THE NONHUMAN ENVIRONMENT.

Effective biophilic design enhances our sense of connection to nature—a relationship fundamental to an idea of community that includes other people as well as the natural environment. Windowless office cubicles, featureless meeting rooms, and isolated dining areas instead typically reinforce feelings of separation and aloneness. Effective biophilic design, in effect, encourages a depth of interaction and collaboration among people and the natural environment that yields a willingness to share knowledge, resources, and skills.

7. BIOPHILIC DESIGN OCCURS IN A MULTIPLICITY OF SETTINGS, INCLUDING INTERIOR, EXTERIOR, AND TRANSITIONAL SPACES AND LANDSCAPES.

Contact with nature in the built environment should occur in a variety of spatial contexts, including interior and exterior settings as well as transitional spaces that connect building interiors with the outside. The beneficial effects of contact with nature tend to increase when interior and exterior environments are connected and even thematically organized. Interior spaces that seem at variance with the outside environment usually breed confusion.

8. EFFECTIVE BIOPHILIC DESIGN INVOLVES AN "AUTHENTIC" EXPERIENCE OF NATURE, RATHER THAN ONE THAT IS ARTIFICIAL OR CONTRIVED.

A successful biophilic experience of nature in the built environment fosters feelings of authenticity and being connected with genuine, and ecologically self-sustaining, natural features and processes. Buildings and landscapes that strike people as artificial and contrived in their natural elements typically exert little lasting benefit over time, and even can provoke scorn and derision. An isolated planter, captive non-native organisms, or artificial furnishings are instead often perceived as inauthentic and artificial.

9. BIOPHILIC DESIGN SEEKS TO ENHANCE THE HUMAN RELATIONSHIP TO NATURAL SYSTEMS AND AVOID ADVERSE ENVIRONMENTAL IMPACTS.

Nature in the built environment strives to be sustainable, in part by minimizing adverse environmental impacts and enhancing the positive human experience of natural systems and processes. Significant construction inevitably results in environmental disturbance in the short term, and, in fact, humans are not the only species to cause these disruptions: certain keystone species such as elephants, alligators, starfish, and other creatures capable of transforming their environment in the process of exploiting it do so as well. The critical challenge is not avoiding significant impacts in the short run, but enhancing the long-term productivity of natural systems (as reflected in measures of biodiversity, biogeochemical cycling, hydrologic regulation, pollination and seed dispersal, decomposition, and other vital ecosystem services). The successful practice of biophilic design seeks to create a more productive, resilient, and self-sustaining natural system that benefits both humans and the nonhuman environment alike. By creating deep, sustained connections to natural features and processes that have proven instrumental in advancing human fitness and survival, biophilic design can create in the modern built environment the best possible habitats for humans: those that advance both health and productivity. In doing so, biophilic design provides long-term benefits to both people and nature.

THREE

THE PRACTICE OF BIOPHILIC DESIGN

Specific design strategies can greatly assist the practice of biophilic design. Many of our greatest historic examples of the successful application of nature in the built environment—some of our most renowned civic and religious structures—were erected without the benefit of professionally trained architects and a list of design approaches. Instead, these buildings relied on a slow, adaptive, and often trial-and-error process of people working in close association with particular physical and social circumstances. But the large-scale and rapid pace of modern construction calls for a more systematic framework. Today's building projects are often hastily and abruptly designed, with a short-term mindset and large-scale footprint. Our mistakes are correspondingly great and not easily rectified. We need guidance and strategies for bringing nature into the built environment.

What are specific strategies for biophilic design? Although these practices provide a kind of practitioners' list, their selection should be cautiously applied and appropriately tailored to the particular uses, conditions, circumstances, history, and culture of a building or constructed landscape. It is also important to recognize that each is somewhat unique. Those seeking to apply strategies for practicing biophilic design should avoid the temptation of a "one size fits all" mentality involving a crude and relatively mindless checklist approach. The identification of particular strategies for the practice of biophilic design does not tell the architect, designer, and developer what to do, but rather what is important, and how one might effectively incorporate nature into the built environment. For these practices to work well, they must be appropriately tailored, interrelated, and integrated into a coherent whole that reflects the particular conditions of a distinctive setting.

With these cautions in mind, I identify and describe here a range of strategies for the practice of biophilic design—including three basic elements and twenty-five associated attributes. Each of the three elements represents fundamental ways that people experience nature: the direct experience of nature, the indirect experience of nature, and the experience of space and place. The twenty-five specific strategies associated with each element involve the actual practice of biophilic design. Illustrations provide context and a diverse set of real-world examples, but there were limits to how many could be selected; therefore they offer only a partial indication of a particular biophilic design practice.

The *direct experience of nature* involves actual contact with basic features and characteristics of the natural environment. These include such naturalistic features as light, air, water, plants, animals, landscapes, weather, views of nature and the outdoors, and fire. A tendency exists to regard biophilic design as involving only the direct experience of nature. Although these features are all important, the direct experience of nature represents only a starting point for effectively engaging with nature in the built environment.

The *indirect experience of nature* relies instead on images or other representations of nature, features of the natural world transformed from their original state, and particular natural patterns and processes that have been especially instrumental in human evolution. The indirect experience of nature often draws on the unique human capacity to convert empirical and objective reality into symbolic and metaphorical forms through projecting thoughts, images, and feelings. Indeed, the symbolic use of nature underlies much of human communication, inventiveness, and the practice of biophilic design.

Providing an indirect experience of nature entails the use of images, pictures, paintings, and other representations of the natural world. The indirect experience of nature also involves the transformation of natural materials such as wood, wool, metal, and leather into an array of products such as coverings, furnishings, and building materials. More subtle patterns and processes occurring in the natural world with special evolutionary significance to people may also be a part of the indirect experience—for example, certain textures, colors, natural geometries, the passage of time, aging, the simulation of light and air, information richness, and the human attempt to mimic the biology and behavior of other organisms (often referred to as biomimicry).

The third basic element of biophilic design is *the experience of space and place*. The spatial setting is the focus here—in effect, the ecological context of the built environment and how people manage and organize their environmental circumstances. Attributes associated with the experience of space and place include prospect and refuge (discerning long distances from a protected and secure space), organized complexity (balancing detail and diversity with order), transitional spaces (linking inside and outside environments as well as interior spaces), mobility (effectively navigating a particular setting), ecological and cultural connections to place, and the integration of parts to wholes. These attributes of space and place reflect how successful human environments—those that promote both good health and greater productivity—depend on the creation of habitats of complementary and connected parts that comprise an overall ecological whole.

How do the human senses fit into this overall formulation? People experience their environment through a variety of senses including sight, sound, touch, smell, taste, time, and movement. Still, in humans the visual is by far the most dominant sense, and it is the primary way that people typically perceive and respond to plants, animals, water, landscapes, and other features of the natural environment. The dominance of the visual sense is due to people having evolved as mainly diurnal creatures highly reliant on sight to discern opportunities and dangers.

When people lack the actual sight of nature—for example, when confined to a windowless space, a barren landscape, or a featureless setting—they often experience confusion and anxiety. Yet despite our inclination to favor the visual sense, the other human senses of touch, smell, taste, sound, time, and movement also remain vital to human welfare and wellbeing. For example, people gravitate not only to the sight of water, but, not unusually, also to its sound, texture, movement, taste, and even smell.

The following description of strategies for the practice of biophilic design does not include a separate category involving the human senses. Instead the senses are a basic characteristic of how all the attributes of nature are experienced—an underlying variable that cuts across strategies of biophilic design. Still, the more senses that are aroused by a particular attribute of the biophilic design, the more likely that it will have effectively incorporated nature into the built environment.

Some caveats: first, this list largely reflects my particular knowledge and experience, although I have certainly been influenced by others. Alternative frameworks have been developed, although the current formulation has benefited in many ways from these other approaches. Second, the rapid development of our knowledge and understanding of the human relation to nature will likely result in further refinements and other revisions in the future. Finally, the order in which these attributes appear does not indicate any priority of importance, and some attributes inevitably overlap and interact with one another.

EXPERIENCES AND ATTRIBUTES OF BIOPHILIC DESIGN

I. Direct Experience of Nature
  1. Light
  2. Air
  3. Water

I. Direct Experience of Nature

1. *Light*

Light is among the most basic aspects of life and human existence. The experience of natural light affects how people respond spatially and temporally, orient themselves to their surroundings, and relate to daylight patterns and shifts in the season. Humans adapt to the shifting conditions of light by responding to changes in weather conditions, the day and evening sky, and what have been called circadian rhythms. These fluctuations in light and dark help people orient themselves within an environment, move across spaces with relative ease and familiarity, experience comfort and good health, and be productive. When the exposure to natural light is impeded by, for example, a windowless space, artificial lighting, or the condition of constant light, people often suffer problems related to health, performance, and wellbeing.

Despite the importance of natural light, a common characteristic of modern construction is the widespread prevalence of artificial lighting in otherwise dark interior spaces. This technological advance has been vital to modern building and construction but it ignores the importance of natural lighting as a basis for human health and performance.

Fortunately, innovative biophilic design can greatly extend the reach of natural lighting deep into building interiors. Design strategies capable of bringing natural lighting into interior spaces often involve glass walls, clerestories, skylights, atria, reflective colors and materials, and mirrors that track the path of sunlight and reflect it into interior areas. Innovative artificial lighting can also mimic the spectral and ambient qualities of natural light.

Beyond simply exposing people to more natural light, biophilic design strategies can enhance the experience by manipulating qualities of light and darkness through varying intensities, the diffusion of light, the presence of light wells, and shadows. In this way, the creative display of natural light can stimulate people's interest, awareness, and knowledge of a space. The Genzyme building in Cambridge, Massachusetts, is a powerful example of how natural light can be imaginatively and technologically brought into interior spaces (Figure 3.1).

2. *Air*

Another fundamental feature of life basic to human existence is the experience of atmospheric conditions. Although air is invisible, and is evident instead through the senses of feel, movement, and smell, the qualities of the air around us are of essential importance. Modern technology has facilitated the ability to control atmospheric conditions, as well as how air is processed even in our largest interior spaces. Yet a growing body of evidence indicates that exposure to constant and processed atmospheric conditions can foster fatigue, impair morale, and compromise health and performance.

Biophilic design strategies for increasing natural ventilation include operable windows, vents, narrower rooms and structures, and chimney stack effects. The simplest way of improving natural ventilation is by increasing access to the outside through balconies, porches, decks, large windows that can be opened, and similar structures.

Natural ventilation can be sometimes simulated by manipulating such basic atmospheric conditions as airflow, temperature, humidity, and barometric pressure. Each condition can create the illusion of a naturally ventilated space. These technological manipulations may not be optimal, although research has revealed that people are still more comfortable and productive—that they experience what some call "thermal pleasure"—under these variable atmospheric conditions than when they are immersed in a constant, fixed atmosphere.

The Alila Hotel in Bali offers an evocative example of the delight and satisfaction that can be obtained from natural ventilation (Figure 3.2).

Figure 3.1. The Genzyme building in Cambridge, Massachusetts, designed by Stefan Behnisch Architects, permits an extraordinary amount of natural light to enter the building, particularly through the central atrium. This remarkable degree of natural light is the result of rooftop heliostat mirrors that track the movement of the sun and reflect its light onto skylight louvers, which in turn channel the light onto interior glass plates hanging at various heights from steel cables like some giant, elegant mobile. The atrium also includes extensive vegetation, small park-like settings, a water feature, and an overall feeling of organized complexity.

Figure 3.2. The Alila Hotel-Uluwatu in Bali, Indonesia, designed by WOHA Architects, provides strong connections between the interior and exterior environments. The structure's ocean views, wood material, reflecting pool, and extensive native plantings enhance the feeling of relationship to nature.

3. *Water*

Water is another basic condition of life and human existence, one that has made the Earth uniquely habitable. Despite its fundamental importance, however, it has become an increasingly hidden and a largely managed resource in the modern built environment. Unfortunately, many view water as a product of technology rather than an experience of nature. Its artificial control has facilitated the construction of enormous buildings with large and dense human aggregations. Yet the experience of water in the built environment has often become separated from the natural world, the result of engineering that encourages people to view this basic element of life as a resource to exploit rather than one to personally experience and celebrate.

Research has revealed that exposure to water can generate significant physical and mental benefits, including stress relief, enhanced performance, and improved problem solving and creativity. The sight of water is visually appealing and capable of engaging a wide variety of other senses including sound, movement, touch, taste, and smell. Water also frequently provides an experience that appeals to a diverse set of biophilic values. Beyond its obvious utility, water is also aesthetically appealing, intellectually stimulating, and emotionally arousing; it also can be a locus of control, a subject of fear, a basis for awe and reverence, and of great symbolic significance. For all of these reasons, the presence of water can transform an otherwise dull and uninspiring environment into one possessing extraordinary appeal and attraction, even if designing a direct water experience into the built environment can be difficult and problematic.

Strategies available for making water more evident include fountains, constructed wetlands, ponds, swales, waterfalls, rainwater spouts, and aquaria. Water is often especially appealing when it is in motion; when it is relatively clear, but contains sufficient nutrients to support life; and when it is capable of engaging a diverse array of senses. Indirect strategies, such as pictures, video, audio technology, and certain patterns and designs can greatly assist the practice of biophilic design.

Two examples from very different parts of the world—the new campus of the University of Nottingham in England and a Buddhist temple complex in Japan—offer striking testimony to the appeal and profound value of water features in the human built environment (Figures 3.3, 3.4).

4. *Plants*

Plants are probably the most frequently employed strategy for creating direct contact between people and nature in the built environment. They are often designed to be a part of landscapes in close proximity to buildings, in building interiors, and in transitional spaces that mark the passage between indoor and outdoor settings. The beneficial effect of plants in the built environment has been highlighted in studies that indicate exposure to plants increases occupant comfort, health, and productivity. Even plants brought into windowless spaces have been found to relieve stress, enhance morale, and improve performance. The therapeutic benefit of plants has long been recognized; consider the tradition of bringing vegetation and flowers into hospitals, hotels, sacred spaces, and other settings.

The field of landscape architecture focuses on plant design in the outside environment near buildings. Few large-scale structures nowadays fail to include some degree of deliberate plant design. But unfortunately, many of these efforts involve highly artificial and contrived designs involving non-native vegetation and plantings and habitats that are formal and require continuous intensive management. A more biophilic and sustainable approach to landscape design would instead emphasize ecologically intact natural systems, native vegetation, and a more naturalistic design.

Plants are among the few living organisms that can be somewhat easily incorporated into building interiors. Effective biophilic design of interior plants should avoid creating

Figure 3.3. The new campus of the University of Nottingham, designed by Michael Hopkins Architects, incorporates a variety of biophilic features that distinguish the buildings and its surrounding space. These include the prominence of wood materials, natural lighting, and an overall sense of connection to the history and geography of the site. The prominence of water particularly provides a central focal point for integrating the space and gives vitality to this former industrial area.

Figure 3.4. Byōdō-in is a Buddhist temple complex located in Kyoto, Japan. Its most renowned building, Phoenix Hall, is a fine example of traditional Japanese architecture with its natural materials and organic shapes and forms. The surrounding pond accentuates the classic beauty of this wooden structure.

contrived and artificial occurrences such as isolated planters consisting of mainly exotic vegetation. Significant advances in knowledge and technology have made it easier to take more ambitious and ecologically innovative approaches to incorporating plants into building interiors. These include, for example, vertically planted or green walls, and large atria with park-like settings.

The effective application of any biophilic design strategy depends on its appropriate, tailored, and integrated use. The beneficial effect of plants is limited when they are placed or integrated in either insufficient or excessive ways. The presence of a single plant rarely exerts much beneficial effect; instead it often becomes a superficial decoration—what could be called a "prisoner plant" that would likely provoke ethical protest if an animal. The excessive and exaggerated occurrence of plants can also lead to perverse consequences, especially when this strategy represents the sole way in which nature is brought into the built environment. Vertical green walls and green roofs, for example, can have little impact when they are at variance with the dominant design features of a space, or when they are largely inaccessible to the building's occupants.

The effective interplay of plants and structures is well defined in Optima Camelview Village, in Scottsdale, Arizona, and can be seen in a vertical facade festooned with plants on a building in Paris. The adjacent building, with its natural materials, indirect experience of nature and nature-based images, and wrought-iron balconies, further enriches the feeling of connection to nature (Figures 3.5, 3.6).

5. *Animals*

Animals have been a prominent and indispensable aspect of people's lives during the long course of human evolution. People coevolved with many creatures that provided food, protection, companionship, and some of our most potent symbols, fantasies, and fears. The continuing significance of animals in modern life is reflected in Americans owning some 150 million cats and dogs, annually visiting zoos and aquariums (more often than all professional baseball, basketball, and football games put together), and adorning our homes and workspaces with images of nature and wildlife. We likely never will encounter a tiger, lion, bear, wolf, panda, or whale, but we continue to insert creatures in our pictures, images, stylized representations, fantasies, and designs. Even animals we largely ignore or fear—such as insects, spiders, and snakes—continue to figure prominently in our images and designs.

The attraction and appeal of animals are deeply embedded in human biology, and so offer a wealth of design opportunities. Yet the occurrence of live animals in the built environment is often logistically and ethically problematic. Some solutions for buildings and constructed landscapes include the installation of ponds, feeders, aviaries, gardens, green roofs, and aquaria, and involve the aid of such modern technologies as web cameras, spotting scopes, and other electronic devices.

A single or a small number of captive animals confined to an isolated location rarely exerts much beneficial impact and can raise legitimate ethical concerns. The inclusion of animals in a biophilic design should, if possible, focus on an abundance of diverse kinds of native species, embedded within an ecosystem of interrelated plants, soils, water, and geological features. Live animals in the built environment should be planned for, and treated with, great care, sensitivity, and ethical restraint.

The most pragmatic approach to incorporating living animals into the modern built environment often involves focusing on the outside landscape—for example, with an aquarium (Figure 3.7). Within the building, it is frequently preferable to rely more on the image, form, and representation of animal life, for instance, with elegant paintings, sculptures, or other adornments (Figure 3.8).

Figure 3.5. Optima Camelview Village, designed and developed by David Hovey, is a residential complex in Scottsdale, Arizona. The development includes extensive vegetation at multiple levels that reinforce the feeling of connection between the built and natural environments. The development's water features, natural materials, and textures further enhance these effects.

Figure 3.6. The vertically planted green wall on the facade of the Musée du quai Branly, designed by Patrick Blanc, inserts green plants into this highly urbanized setting. The adjacent building, although it lacks living organisms, subtly enhances this biophilic quality by virtue of its organic shapes and forms, natural materials, and natural geometries. The juxtaposition of all these elements elicits the human affinity for nature.

Figure 3.7. The fish, coral, and other aquatic organisms in this aquarium at the Smilow Cancer Center in New Haven, Connecticut, provide patients and staff with physical and mental relief in a highly stressful setting. Research has revealed that such tanks can provide substantial therapeutic benefits. Yet the healing effect is often minimized if the tank is isolated or at variance with other predominant features of a designed space.

Figure 3.8. The hand-forged bronze peacock doors at the Palmer House in Chicago, Illinois, designed by Louis Comfort Tiffany, are a lovely example of animal images used to enliven and enrich an essentially dark interior space.

6. Landscapes

Landscape design in close proximity to buildings and occasionally within building interiors is both a vital element of built environments as well as a common strategy for facilitating contact between people and nature in those environments. Careful planning and construction are required, however, to keep landscaping from becoming a largely superficial decoration rather than a meaningful experience of the natural world. We all have walked through and around uninspired landscape designs involving just a few high-maintenance non-native plant species. By contrast, an effective biophilic landscape can often exert more than a superficial effect on the people who experience it.

Certain landscape designs affect people because of their importance during the course of human evolution. These include spreading shrubs and trees, colorful foliage and flowers, the presence of water, long-prospect views, sheltered spaces, prominent trees, natural pathways, savannah-like settings, open understories, and forested edges. Studies indicate that even ordinary natural scenes depicting a coherent and ecologically connected landscape are generally more appealing to people than landscapes with artificial surfaces, few and exotic plants, an absence of geological features, and the dominance of human-made artifacts.

The most effective biophilic landscapes, then, are generally comprised of interconnected soils, waters, plants, animals, and geological forms revealed in a space that is ecologically coherent. These integrated and typically more resilient landscapes usually have high levels of biodiversity, tend to be self-sustaining, and satisfy a variety of ecosystem needs such as pollination, seed dispersal, decomposition, and pollution control.

Biophilic landscape designs can take many forms, including constructed wetlands, ponds, grasslands, prairies, forests, and other habitats. These landscapes are often enhanced by the presence of pathways, viewing areas, observational platforms, and other means for people to engage with, and participate in, the experience of natural systems and processes.

The biophilic design of interior landscapes often focuses on atria, courtyards, entry areas, hallways, meeting rooms, and dining areas. The ability to design interior landscapes has advanced considerably due to our expanded knowledge of the field and to technologies that control light, air, water, humidity, soils, and varied types of plant- and animal-related materials. Creating interior park-like settings of beauty, diversity, interest, and comfort can contribute to the productivity of those who inhabit these spaces. These landscape designs should avoid, however, being isolated or at variance with the dominant design features of interior spaces or they will become increasingly ignored and neglected over time.

Evocative landscapes in the built environment can be expansive, with sweeping views, or intimate, as in a Japanese garden (Figure 3.9).

7. Weather

A fundamental aspect of the human experience of nature is exposure to weather. Human adaptation and response to weather have been critical in people's survival and history. Even today, people dwell to an exceptional degree on the qualities and conditions of weather. The human response to sunshine, rain, wind, temperature, and other meteorological conditions remains deeply embedded in biology and consciousness. Apart from its historic significance, weather still very much controls our capacity to grow food, secure access to potable water, and promote our safety and security.

Still, the built environment retains an ambivalent relationship to weather. A major historic motivation for constructing larger, more technologically sophisticated, and secure buildings was the desire to remove people from the challenges and vagaries of weather, insulating us from the dangers and uncertainties of storms, excessive cold and heat, and un-

Figure 3.9. Japanese gardens are often aesthetically compelling and calming landscapes. These garden designs typically employ an idealized and abstract conception of nature, as reflected in the miniaturization of plants, the emphasis on particular vantage points, and a highly stylized approach. Visitors nonetheless often feel serenity, peace, and a sense of natural beauty in these gardens.

expected events by creating consistent atmospheric conditions within these constructed environments. As in many other areas of modern life, our efforts may have been too successful. Highly insulated buildings can dull the senses and separate us from one of the most fundamental ways in which humans experience nature.

Two examples, the Ponta dos Ganchos resort in Brazil and the glass house near Tokyo, illustrate how an interior space can have a powerful connection to outside weather conditions (Figures 3.10, 3.11).

People benefit from knowing the meteorological conditions of their external environment, including the quality of sunlight, the likelihood of fair or foul conditions, and other aspects of weather. When denied access and awareness of weather, many people become anxious and disoriented. By contrast, the architect Kevin Nute (2004) points out the advantages of remaining aware of the weather: "Rethinking the way buildings interact with weather could not only help us to remain more alert and content during the long periods we spend indoors but also increase our awareness of our interdependence with the natural world" (p. 3).

The satisfying experience of weather is often associated with small-scale construction, but it can also be designed into larger-scale buildings. Strategies for enhancing exposure to weather include operable windows, views, porches, balconies, decks, terraces, courtyards, and other inside and outside connections to the outdoor environment. Transparent roofs, rainwater collectors and spouts, visible storm runoff, the sound of wind, and the movement of water can also enhance a greater awareness of meteorological conditions. Simulating the experience of weather can be the product of manipulating sunlight, airflow, humidity, temperature, and barometric pressure.

Figure 3.10. Ponta dos Ganchos resort in Brazil incorporates several biophilic design attributes that enhance its appeal. These include reminders of the intimate relationship of land and sea, striking ocean views, an abundance of natural materials, close connection between the interior and exterior outside environments, and areas of prospect and refuge.

Figure 3.11. The glass house near Tokyo designed by Kengo Kuma powerfully links the building's interior with its exterior setting. The prominence of water, natural lighting and ventilation, and a feeling of connection to weather further enhance this biophilic effect.

8. *Views*

A view of nature is a frequently employed strategy for enriching a sense of contact between people and the natural world. These sights can enrich a distant horizon: consider the prominent landscape features of a seashore, mountain, or an unusual stand of trees. Yet despite its importance and appeal, this form of contact between people and nature can also be limiting in terms of engagement and immersion. For a view of nature to be deeply satisfying and beneficial, it often needs to simultaneously engage people in complementary ways.

Views of nature generally exert their greatest impact when they are at relatively moderate to short distances, at modest heights, and from sheltered spaces. Even the view of a beautiful natural setting can be undermined by an excessively high viewing area, especially when that location lacks an external ledge, shelf, or projection that could mitigate the transition from a high inside view to a steep sweeping outside environment. Many people harbor ambivalent feelings about great heights; in fact, a fear of heights is a common phobia, along with such other environmental aversions as snakes, spiders, bees, and lightning. Great heights can yield awe-inspiring views, but also foster anxiety and intimidation. These adverse effects can be reduced by such design strategies as balconies, decks, ledges, and sheltered spaces.

Views of nature should avoid degraded natural systems or artificially created environments, though effective views can also complement and connect with interior spaces that feature a biophilic design. By contrast, a bland and artificial interior at variance with a beautiful outside view can frequently be dissatisfying and frustrating.

The power of a beautiful view of nature is reflected in the connections among materials, water, and the viewscape at the Fregate Island Resort in the Seychelles (Figures 3.12, 3.13).

9. *Fire*

Fire may seem like an odd attribute of direct biophilic design since its occurrence is typically the consequence of deliberate human intervention and it is often associated with environmental harm and destruction. Natural fires—caused by lightning, volcanic action, and other forms of spontaneous combustion—are often perceived as a destructive force. Despite these misgivings, the exploitation and control of fire represents one of the most significant developments in human history, one that fundamentally distinguished us from other life. The progressive control of fire became the basis for the human production of energy, food, heat, and light as it transformed resources from one state into another. The awareness and response to fire consequently became deeply embedded in the human consciousness. An inherent human affinity for fire emerged not only as a practical necessity, but also as a powerful facet of human imagination and creativity.

But contemporary life and the modern built environment have largely obscured and marginalized the experience of fire. Its vital significance has frequently receded from our awareness. We may enjoy the occasional sight and comfort of a fireplace, although this form of contact with nature has become largely decorative, but in most large-scale modern construction, the experience of fire is rarely evident.

The actual and symbolic experience of fire, nonetheless, continues to generate significant satisfaction and benefits. Beyond the actual sight of fire, its appearance can be suggested by the presence of hearth-like areas that encourage relaxation and intimacy. Certain shapes and colors that add vitality to building forms, fabrics, and other interior design can suggest the qualities of fire. We can further enhance an awareness and appreciation of fire by making it more visible and recognizable in the built environment. For example, rather than concealing the properties of fire associated with heating, cooking, and energy production, these benefits can be rendered more explicitly apparent.

Figure 3.12 and Figure 3.13. The Fregate Island Resort in the Seychelles Islands includes many biophilic features that contribute to its special appeal. These include extensive use of natural materials, the presence of water, outstanding views, areas of prospect and refuge, and a strong sense of connection to place.

The powerful appeal of a fireplace consisting of wood or stone is revealed in Figures 3.14 and 3.15.

II. Indirect Experience of Nature

10. *Images*

Images of nature are an ancient means for bringing the likeness of the natural world into the built environment. Images of nature in building interiors can be traced back to the cave paintings of Spain's Altamira and of France's Chauvet and Lascaux caverns, the petroglyphs of Australia and India, and other early imagery. The actual and fanciful depiction of nature has long exerted lasting and profound impressions. The anthropologist and veterinarian Elizabeth Lawrence (1993), reflecting on the importance of such symbolic images, observed: "The human need for metaphorical expression finds its greatest fulfillment through reference to [nature and especially] the animal kingdom. No other realm affords such vivid expression of symbolic concepts" (p. 113).

Powerful examples of images and likenesses of nature that enhance our exposure to the natural world include the Norwich Cathedral Rectory in Norwich, England, a wooden door of the Bristol Cathedral, and a traditional Japanese interior (Figures 3.16, 3.17, 3.18).

Literal and metaphorical images of nature are often encountered in civic, educational, and religious architecture. Images of plants, animals, water, landscapes, and geological features continue to be common forms of contact between people and nature in the built environment. Although many contemporary sterile, lifeless buildings lack even this degree of exposure with nature, such images remain a frequently used strategy for enhancing contact with nature, sometimes even by employing the media of photography, computer, and video. Studies have revealed that the more isolated people are from nature

Figure 3.14. The Post Ranch Inn in Big Sur, California, largely designed by Mickey Muennig, contains various biophilic features that largely account for its attraction and success. These include the extensive use of natural materials, views of the nearby ocean, fireplace and hearth-like settings, prominent elements of prospect and refuge, a feeling of connection to the ecology of place, and the use of natural geometries.

Figure 3.15. This fireplace in a home on Martha's Vineyard, Massachusetts, designed by Lew French, combines natural materials, particularly wood and stone, to create a comforting and aesthetically pleasing effect. The intimacy provided by the fireplace and hearth is reinforced by the use of local natural materials and the structure's overall design.

Figure 3.16. The renovated rectory dining area at Norwich Cathedral, Norwich, England, designed by Michael Hopkins Architects, employs several biophilic design strategies to enhance its appeal. These include a reliance on natural materials, especially juxtaposed wood and stone, natural geometries, organized complexity, and a feeling of connection to place.

Figure 3.17. This interior wooden church door at Bristol Cathedral in Bristol, England, is especially pleasing. Its effect stems from such biophilic features as wood carvings and natural color contrasts. Organic shapes and sinuous natural geometries further inspire the carved images.

Figure 3.18. The appeal of traditional Japanese interior architecture reflects the influence of several biophilic properties. These include the widespread use of natural materials, a feeling of aging and time, areas of prospect and refuge, and a strong sense of connection to place. The tatami mats accentuate these effects, which are further enhanced by diffuse natural lighting and the linking of transitional spaces.

in the built environment, such as working in windowless spaces, the more likely they are to insert pictures of the natural world into their immediate surroundings. Additionally, contemporary fabrics and interior designs frequently employ both objective and highly stylized images of nature.

Indoors, people often maintain contact with nature through actual and fantasized depictions of the natural world, which they display in paintings, photographs, sculptures, fabric designs, and calendars. A casual review of personal residences, healthcare facilities, educational institutions, office buildings, religious structures, and hospitality centers reveals an extraordinary array of images of nature. The creatures depicted include dogs, cats, cows, horses, lions, tigers, whales, bears, giraffes, all sorts of birds and fish, butterflies, bees, dinosaurs, dragons, and cartoon characters, as well as trees, ferns, bushes, flowers, and mushrooms.

The varied incorporation of plants and animals in capital columns offers a good example of nature's images adorning building supports and structures (Figure 3.19).

The physical and psychological effects of representations of nature remain somewhat uncertain. Some studies suggest that images of nature add beauty and color, contribute to stress relief, and generally enhance occupant health and productivity. Yet images of nature can be superficial and transient, lacking the necessary engagement, involvement, and immersion to exert a lasting impact. Moreover, the occurrence of only a small number of isolated images of nature, unconnected to other design features of a space, often results in little significant improvement in people's physical and mental health and wellbeing.

Three conditions appear to substantially enhance the positive influence that nature-based images can have on the people viewing them. First, the images should be sufficiently prolific and diverse rather than focus on a single species or landscape. Second, these images should include a diversity of human experiences and experiences in nature.

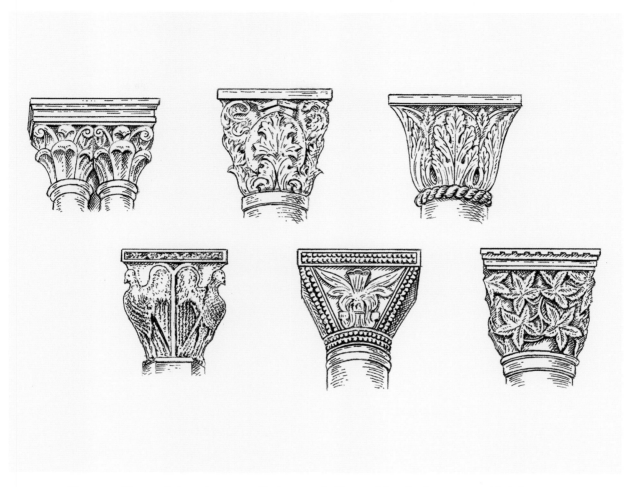

Figure 3.19. These capitals, resting on top of columns and pillars, enrich and enliven a space with their nature-based images, including leaves, ferns, and birds. Although these forms often are not exact replicas, and instead are products of human creation inspired by nature, they can transform a post from a simple inanimate object to a dynamic, lifelike entity.

Finally, these images should create a thematic whole rather than represent isolated or random features of the natural world.

Representations of nature can be fantastic or realistic, a product of human imagination as much as an objective and empirical reality. Nonetheless, imaginary depictions of nature need to possess elements of "authenticity" that embody the actual properties of the natural world. Fanciful designs inspired by living nature should strive, for example, to capture characteristics of actual growth and the natural geometry characteristic of organic forms. The art historian Owen Jones (1986) concluded that many designs are often inspired by images of nature, brilliantly stating: "In the best periods of art all ornament was rather based upon an observation of the principles which regulate the arrangement of form in nature, than on an attempt to imitate the absolute forms of those works … True art consists in idealizing, and not copying, the forms of nature" (p. 2).

An evocative, powerful example of a fanciful arboreal image of nature is revealed in a window sculpture at the Ronald Reagan Airport in Washington, D.C., designed by Kent Bloomer (Figure 3.20).

11. *Materials*

Natural materials are often an effective means for inserting indirect contact with nature into the built environment. Natural materials possess visual and tactile qualities that few if any artificial materials can replicate. Whether used as building materials, furnishings, fabrics, or art, these materials are often so transformed from their original state that their natural origins can be difficult to determine. Still, physical and psychological exposure to natural materials typically evokes a strong, and frequently deeply satisfying and beneficial, human response.

Three examples of the effective use of natural materials are drawings of balcony and building facades in Paris; a traditional building in Provence; and the biophilic design fea-

Figure 3.20. This arboreal window sculpture designed by Kent Bloomer, at the Ronald Reagan Airport in Washington, D.C., provides a powerful connection between the interior space and the natural world beyond. The plantlike form does not occur in nature, yet its shape captures the authentic qualities and metabolic growth patterns of living nature, helping to invigorate its space.

tures of a church facade in New Haven, Connecticut. These scenes can elicit an almost palpable sense of nature in the built environment (Figures 3.21, 3.22, 3.23).

A wide spectrum of natural materials is used in the built environment, including wood, stone, and clay (Figures 3.24, 3.25). The appeal of natural materials reflects the influence of many factors, including the capacity to evoke a variety of senses. The natural geometries the materials possess, such as fractals, are especially alluring. In this regard, each instance of a material is fundamentally like other occurrences of the same substance, yet at the same time represents an infinitely diverse variation of a basic pattern or theme. For example, all panels of the same species of an oak floor may look alike, yet on close inspection they are each subtly different from the other. Natural materials reveal the properties of maturation, aging, and change in adaptive response to the challenges of survival over time. By contrast, artificial materials often lack dynamic features; instead they seem fixed in lifeless space and time.

12. *Texture*

Texture refers to the feel, appearance, and arrangement of parts in relation to one another in the built environment. Important biophilic properties of texture highlight the size, shape, tactile quality, and proportion of a building or landscape. People experience texture visually and through a variety of their other senses.

Texture is often confused with the sensory experience of touching natural materials. Yet the experience of texture typically extends beyond materials to other forms of contact with nature, including light, color, and sound as reflected in certain rhythms and harmonies.

The glass dome at the Palace of Music in Barcelona exemplifies the use of light and color to express texture, whereas a stone wall in New Haven, Connecticut, begs to have one touch its rough surface (Figures 3.26, 3.27).

Figure 3.21. This balcony and building facade are characteristic of traditional Parisian architecture. Biophilic qualities that contribute to its special aesthetic attraction include organic imagery, naturalistic stone relief, nature-inspired metal carvings, fractal geometry, and natural materials.

Figure 3.22. This modest building in Provence, France, includes several biophilic features that transform the structure from a simple to a more complex and appealing construction. These include the red roof tile, brick and wood materials, earth-tone colors, natural textures, integration with the surrounding landscape, and pronounced sense of place.

Figure 3.23. This pediment, part of a church facade in New Haven, Connecticut, includes biophilic features that transform a simple structure into a more detailed, interesting, and appealing one. These include leaf and fernlike relief, triangular rising geometry and curves, information richness, and organized complexity.

Figure 3.24. This simple fountain in a small English town in the Cotswolds contains powerful biophilic elements that help account for its appeal. These include the natural materials and textures, moving and falling water, and organic stonework.

Figure 3.25. Framing this wooden door at Yale University in New Haven, Connecticut, with stone created an aesthetically and emotionally effective design. Its attraction derives from such biophilic features as contrasting natural materials, a curved arch, contrasting natural colors, and organized complexity.

Figure 3.26. The Palace of Music in Barcelona contains a remarkably lovely and centrally situated colored glass dome designed by Antoni Rigalt. Specific biophilic features that contribute to the appeal of this inverted glass fixture include brilliant gold and blue colors that imply the sun and the sky, the dome's curved surface, diffuse natural lighting, and organic images such as the rosettes.

Figure 3.27. The bark of a tree alongside a stone wall in New Haven, Connecticut, contains a number of arresting biophilic features. These include natural geometries, especially fractals; different textures and natural materials; and a sense of connection to place. The stone and bark are contrasting materials, but share the similar biophilic property of predictable change associated with an overall underlying pattern. The combined effect offers stimulation and detail, yet in a coherent and connected fashion.

Natural textures in the built environment are often most apparent in building facades, flooring, walls, landscapes, and water features. People generally prefer natural over artificial textures because natural textures historically have helped advance human safety and security. For example, smooth and wavy textures generally signify secure circumstances, while rough and unfinished surfaces suggest unknown and risky conditions. People generally tolerate a greater degree of unfinished and variable texture on building exteriors than in interior built spaces.

13. *Color*

Color is an especially salient aspect of how humans connect the natural and constructed worlds. Its significance reflects the role that color played for early humans as a primarily diurnal species that depended on color to help its members locate food and water, move safely within their environment, identify dangers and opportunities, and order and organize their natural and human-constructed settings. Color's inherent appeal can be so strong that even the most hardened individual finds it difficult to remain indifferent to a colorful rainbow, beautiful flower, or spectacular sunset. We feel as though we are looking at the sky rather than a blue stucco wall in Figure 3.28.

Color can be especially important in identifying and differentiating objects from one another. Its presence can often convert a complex and confusing scene into one with structure and coherence. For example, an undifferentiated landscape or even streetscape can become meaningful by the presence of a colorful natural or simulated environmental feature, which can help transform an otherwise dull and lifeless space into one that seems distinctive and alive in both quality and appearance.

Yet today color is often misused and inappropriately applied, so that it seems strident and excessive. For example, modern technology has permitted the production of just about any color, often resulting in its injudicious and discomforting application. In-

Figure 3.28. The pale blue of this stucco wall helps transform it from a simple object to one possessing vitality and a skylike image. The flowers below and window above enhance the biophilic effect.

ordinately bright and contrasting colors can even cause "vibrating" colors that can have a stressful effect on the viewer.

The theory of ecological color valence suggests that people generally prefer natural colors that have proven advantageously appealing to humans over time. These colors are frequently the blues associated with clear skies and clean water, and the greens of vascular plants that suggest flowering and fruiting bodies. By contrast, research has revealed consistently negative responses associated with the browns and purples of rotting food and fecal matter.

The challenge of effectively applying color underscores the reality that any biophilic design feature can be either appropriately used or poorly applied. Yet the frequent misuse of color should not preclude the recognition that color remains an important technical biophilic design strategy. It should encourage instead a cautious approach to its technical application that generally favors blues, greens, and other earth tones.

14. *Shapes and Forms*

Natural shapes and forms are among the most enduring and powerful ways of bringing nature into the built environment. Including them in landscapes, exteriors, or interiors sometimes means incorporating a fairly precise and empirical depiction of nature. Yet these shapes and forms inspired by nature, especially living organisms, can also be more a product of human imagination and creativity, rather than exact replicas of those encountered in the natural world.

Naturalistic shapes and forms can occur on building facades, in interior spaces, and in the patterns of fabrics and furnishings. Their frequent occurrence adds vitality to otherwise largely lifeless settings, helping transform inanimate and static structures into ones that possess naturalistic and ambient qualities.

This application of biophilic design can elicit the likeness of organic life, through the occurrence of biomorphic architecture that will be more fully described in Chapter 4. This incorporation of the shapes and forms of nature is illustrated by the colorful onion-like curves of the Kremlin's Saint Basil's Cathedral in Moscow, the Sydney Opera House in Australia, and the Gothic architecture of Yale University's residential Branford College (Figures 3.29, 3.30, 3.31).

A resurgent interest in organic architecture likely reflects a revived desire to bring the shapes of nature into the built environment. This focus marks a shift away from the artificial and sterile geometries and lifeless forms of so-called International Architecture. Especially prominent examples include the work of Frank Gehry, Zaha Hadid, and others. This change is certainly laudable. Yet these organic designs often remain in many ways disconnected from nature, especially in their interior spaces (see Chapter 4). They often seem more sculptural than ecological without a sincere biophilic attempt at bringing nature into the built environment in an integrated way. The Sydney Opera House represents a fine example of bringing the shapes and forms of nature into the built environment. Yet in many ways it stands apart from the culture and ecology of its surroundings, as Figure 3.30 illustrates.

15. *Information Richness*

Nature's information richness and detail are among its most distinguishing characteristics. Even in our modern information age, the natural world likely constitutes the most information-rich environment people ever encounter. Nature's detail and diversity have been linked to the development of the human capacities for rational thinking, problem solving, curiosity, and creativity.

Information richness in the built environment can be a satisfying source of intellectual stimulation and emotional satisfaction. People generally prefer detail and diversity in both natural and built settings over homogeneity, sameness, and uniformity. Built en-

Figure 3.29. Saint Basil's Cathedral in Moscow symbolizes Russia's spiritual and secular power. The shape and color of its onion domes, which give the illusion of flames reaching to the sky, are inspired by nature, as are its natural geometries.

Figure 3.30. The Opera House in Sydney, Australia, designed by Jørn Utzon, has become iconic of modern organic architecture. Its most distinctive feature is the shell-like spherical forms that remind people of bird wings or a bird-of-paradise plant. The building's location astride the city harbor further enhances the biophilic effect, though the limitations of its organic design are revealed in the structure's relative lack of connections to other biophilic features and processes.

Figure 3.31. A Yale University undergraduate residential college includes many of the biophilic characteristics found in Gothic architecture. These include widespread natural materials, particularly stone, metal, and slate; organic shapes and forms; curved arches; naturalistic reliefs; and areas of prospect and refuge. Despite the extraordinary detail and diversity found in most Gothic structures, the overall effect is often orderly and coherent.

vironments should foster curiosity, exploration, discovery—even the experience of mystery and surprise. Natural imagery in interior and exterior settings can foster variety and stimulation. Yet to avoid chaos and confusion, interior and exterior environments should be orderly, coherent, and organized.

Buildings and landscapes that are information-rich because of the actual or simulated inclusion of natural features, such as those often encountered in Paris, tend to exude qualities of abundance and detail in many settings—for instance, they may be particularly ornate, multidimensional, and fractal-like—and to include both living and nonliving natural materials. A similar pattern can be encountered in Yale's Gothic architecture.

16. *Change, Age, and the Patina of Time*

Change, age, and the patina of time are basic features of natural and living systems. The natural world is never static; instead it is subject to pressures that lead to an almost constant state of flux and adaptation. Organic life moves through metabolic stages of inception, maturation, senescence, death, and decomposition. The word *metabolism* derives from the Greek term for change.

A fundamental objective of buildings and human construction has been to resist change, especially the corrosive forces of nature. But the attempt to deny change in nature can become excessive and dysfunctional. People need to be exposed to the dynamic forces of the natural world, so they can become aware of and participate in the processes of maturation and adaptation. The absence of change intimates an absence of life, and fosters feelings of monotony and boredom.

Designs that lack a sense of maturation, including the weathering effects of time and the vicissitudes of adaptation to changed circumstances, strike most people as artificial and inauthentic. By contrast a structure or material that yields to changing circumstances—a building that might have once housed a butcher's shop and is now an electronics store; a wooden beam converted to a modern furnishing; or stones and bricks reused as modern construction materials—are both aesthetically appealing and provide a host of practical benefits. Sustainability is also about caring for and keeping objects rather than carelessly discarding them. Recycled elements of the built environment can not only lessen the ecological footprint of modern life, but also often add grace and beauty.

An older facade along a canal in Amsterdam illustrates how change and the patina of time are striking with their powerful beauty, all while promoting a lasting sustainability (Figure 3.32).

17. *Natural Geometries*

Natural geometries refer to mathematical properties often encountered in nature that have a special role in human evolution and development. Instilling these mathematical properties in the built environment helps to promote feelings of balance, symmetry, and harmony. The Chhatrapati Shivaji International Airport Terminal 2 in Mumbai, India, is a good example (Figure 3.33).

The tulip staircase in the Queen's House in Greenwich, England, also shows how a natural geometric form creates a profoundly moving interior space (Figure 3.34).

A prominently occurring geometric pattern often encountered in both nature and built environments is hierarchically organized scales. For example, most trees contain a broad base that supports progressively narrower, higher levels in a mathematically proportionate manner. Sinuous shapes and curves are another natural geometric pattern that suggest the adaptive response of living and nonliving features to changing conditions and circumstances over time. By contrast, many modern structures rely excessively—and unappealingly—on straight-line, sharply angled, box-like geometries that appear to be rigidly imposed on their spaces.

Another important natural geometry is the occurrence of fractals. A fractal is a basic

Figure 3.32. This scene from Amsterdam evokes a strong sense of place. Various biophilic features contribute to this feeling, including compatible connections of land and water, the patina of aging and the passing of time, naturalistic colors, natural geometries, and an evocation of the culture and ecology of the Dutch lowlands.

Figure 3.33. The biophilic effect of the Chhatrapati Shivaji International Airport, Terminal 2, in Mumbai, India, designed by SOM Architects, is largely due to its organic forms, natural geometries, long vistas, spaciousness, and natural lighting.

Figure 3.34. The tulip staircase in the Queen's House in Greenwich, England, designed by Inigo Jones, has an arresting aesthetic effect. Its most outstanding biophilic feature is the nautilus-shell-like spiral of the circular stairs. Other biophilic attributes contributing to its appeal include the organic images in its metal railing, natural geometries, diffuse natural light, and its marble and stone floor.

pattern or shape repeated in continuously changing yet predictable ways. The architect Nikos Salingaros (2015) explains: "A fractal contains well-defined subdivisions of structure in an ordered hierarchy of scales" (p. 15). Fractal patterns can be seen in the slightly differing yet fundamentally similar leaves of a single tree, or the ever-smaller branches of a broccoli or cauliflower. The 2016 book *Fractal Worlds* by Michael Frame and Amelia Urry elucidates this concept as similar or repeating patterns of many shapes in nature, which when seen under magnification or at great scale can reveal many layers of symmetry to create a sense of wholeness. Examples abound of fractals in the construction of the built environment as well, with many appealing building and fabric designs, many historic, using fractal geometry to include patterns that frequently vary, but in a somewhat anticipated fashion. Fractal geometry also occurs in some of our most attractive and engaging landscapes and neighborhoods.

An especially prominent fractal can be found in the extraordinary ceiling of the Charleston Unitarian Church (Figure 3.35). In a more mundane but frequently experienced example, the persistent appeal of many Paris neighborhoods is due to their fractal geometries, whereby a basic building pattern of one is varied slightly, and in proportion, to complement nearby structures (Figure 3.36).

A final natural geometry is the so-called Fibonacci sequence. This mathematical sequence involves adding two numbers to get the next in the sequence: for instance, the series 1, 2, 3, 5, 8, is a Fibonacci sequence because the sum of the first two numbers, 1 and 2, is 3; the sum of the 2 and 3 is 5; and the sum of the 3 and 5 is 8 (and so on). This sequence is evident in many living forms, such as the branching of trees, the arrangement of leaves on a stem, the fruitlets of a pineapple, the flowering of an artichoke, the uncurling of a fern, the arrangement of a pine cone, and the family tree of honeybees (Jones and Wilson 2006; Brousseau 1969). Perhaps the most renowned fractal form in the built environment is the Taj Mahal (Figure 3.37).

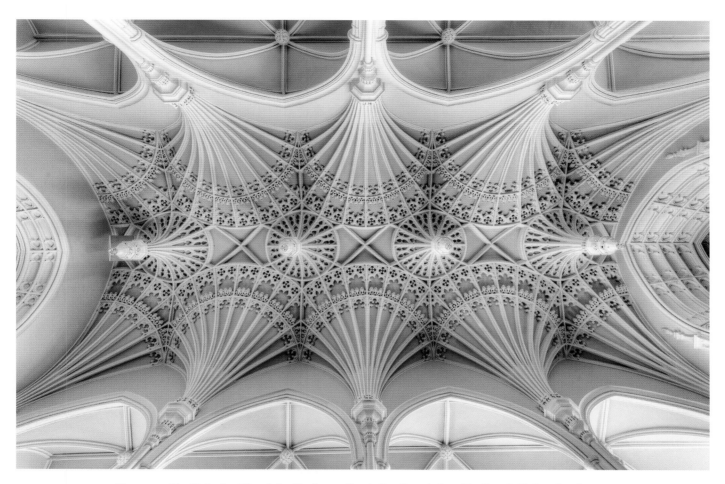

Figure 3.35. The Unitarian Church in Charleston, South Carolina, designed by Francis D. Lee, is a fine example of the biophilic roots of much sacred architecture. Its biophilic features include the ornate ceiling with its organic shapes and forms, natural materials, information richness, and organized complexity.

Figure 3.36. The enduring appeal of Paris partly and significantly derives from the many biophilic features of its buildings and neighborhoods. These biophilic design attributes include the widespread presence of masonry and iron work that incorporate images inspired by nature, the extensive use of natural materials, the subtle occurrence of similar yet highly diverse natural geometries such as fractals, a strong connection to place, information richness, and organized complexity.

Figure 3.37. The extraordinary appeal of the Taj Mahal, in Agra, India, is partially due to its many prominent biophilic features. These include the structure's natural geometries, organic forms, natural materials, presence of water, and an overall harmonious shape that incorporates a diversity of details.

Artificial lighting and processed air have allowed modern society to construct structures of immense size, and rendered even the most interior spaces habitable nearly any time of day, and in any weather or season. It has also contributed to building occupants being disconnected from sunlight, natural patterns, circadian rhythms, diurnal cycles, normal atmospheric conditions, and weather. The assumption is that people can function effectively under these circumstances, and that humans, being not just another biological animal, do not require a sensory-rich and stimulating environment to be healthy, productive, and well. But recent research suggests otherwise. People subject to continuous artificial lighting, processed air, and other forms of unnatural lighting and atmospheric conditions appear less motivated, experience greater symptoms of illness, and perform less optimally.

Although the economic, technological, and logistical advantages of widespread artificial lighting and processed air make it very likely that we will continue our widespread reliance on them for the foreseeable future, simulating natural lighting and atmospheric conditions can help mitigate these negative effects.

A hospital waiting room at the University of California at Davis is exemplary in its use of simulated natural lighting to create a peaceful and calming setting (Figure 3.38). And by using filtered natural lighting and other elements inspired by the outdoors, a beloved reading room at a Yale University library offers a peaceful, contemplative place to learn (Figure 3.39).

One promising strategy is to replicate the spectral and dynamic qualities of natural lighting. This practice includes mimicking the variability of daytime conditions by shifting light intensity and even duplicating the scattering effects of altering light and passing clouds. It is also possible to enhance the dynamic qualities of natural lighting by adjusting the so-called color temperature of light as it strikes the human eye.

Processed air can also be manipulated and controlled to mimic outside atmospheric conditions. This approach adjusts airflow, temperature, humidity, and barometric pressure. Innovative heating, ventilation, and cooling systems can further simulate natural atmospheric conditions, producing what has been referred to as thermal delight.

These innovative technologies should be encouraged, but more direct and often architectural means (both traditional and modern) also exist for capturing exterior natural lighting and air conditions and bringing these attributes of nature into building interiors. Examples of often effective techniques include operable windows, vents, airshafts, porches, light wells, clerestories, glass walls, and light colors.

19. *Biomimicry*

The term *biomimicry* can denote the adoption of distinctive features of other species to serve human needs. This means of bringing nature into the built environment is related but somewhat different from biophilia. Biomimicry emphasizes other species' unique biological features, whereas biophilia focuses on human evolved adaptive responses to the natural world that became genetically encoded because they advanced people's fitness and survival. In other words, biophilia is about human adaptive and biological responses to nature, whereas biomimicry stresses the evolved characteristics of nonhuman creatures whose patterns and strategies have become exploited for human purposes.

Biophilia and biomimicry strongly share, however, an admiration for the wisdom and ingenuity of nature, and they can both enhance human health and wellbeing. For example, the biomimetic understanding of creatures like termites and spiders can improve the efficiency of climatic controls and the structural strength of building materials. From

Figure 3.38. This hospital waiting room at the University of California, Davis, employs a variety of biophilic strategies to create a comfortable and calming setting. Despite an interior space that lacks natural lighting, compensating biophilic attributes include widespread use of natural materials, simulated natural lighting, earth-tone colors, a feeling of spaciousness, and areas of prospect and refuge.

Figure 3.39. This library reading room at Yale University contains several biophilic features that contribute to its appeal. These include the widespread use of natural materials, filtered natural light, organic fixtures, colored glass forms, and other naturalistic colors.

a biophilic perspective, this knowledge can be of great practical significance, although given our own evolution it is unlikely to alter most humans' inherent aversion to these particular creatures.

Biophilia and biomimicry also converge in their appreciation and respect for nature's wisdom, and in the fact that nature has yielded extraordinarily diverse solutions to the challenges faced by humans and nonhumans alike as they seek to survive and thrive in their habitats. Every species represents an eloquent biological solution no less astonishing than our own. We are inspired by the creative genius of other life, as Janine Benyus (2008), the pioneer of biomimicry, eloquently articulated: "The conscious emulation of life's genius is a natural part of biophilia ... [We are] drawn to life's mastery and to try, with equal parts of awe and envy, to do what birds and fish and insects do ... The act of asking nature's advice, of valuing nature for its wisdom, bridges the distance that has developed between humans and the rest of life. In this way, biomimicry is a process of homecoming akin to biophilia" (p. 40).

Two examples of biomimetic building design are the Beijing National Stadium ("Bird's Nest") built for the 2008 Summer Olympics, and the Supertree Grove in Gardens by the Bay Park in Singapore (Figures 3.40, 3.41).

III. Experience of Space and Place

20. *Prospect and Refuge*

Prospect and refuge are two complementary biophilic design attributes that speak to people's evolutionary preferences for certain spatial conditions. Prospect focuses on the perception of long distances, whereas refuge provides enclosed spaces that afford greater intimacy, protection, and security. Long vistas facilitate the recognition of distant threats and opportunities, while refuge affords the safety of observing these options from relatively secure and sheltered spaces.

People covet the complementary combination of prospect and refuge. In building interiors, this inclination is satisfied by long views from an office, meeting, or living space. In exterior settings, strategies such as porches, balconies, decks, courtyards, and colonnades can facilitate the experience of prospect and refuge.

Within building interiors, prospect and refuge can be achieved by visually connecting spaces. For example, sight lines can tie rooms together rather than walling them off from one another. The pioneering architect Frank Lloyd Wright emphasized this value of prospect and refuge, advocating for "breaking the box" as a visual strategy for connecting interior spaces. Many contemporary designs stress open floor plans that favor long visual sight lines, although these approaches often neglect the equally important significance of complementary refuge spaces. The Jardines de Mexico Hill Restaurant near Cuernavaca, Mexico, is a compelling and attractive example of prospect and refuge (Figure 3.42).

21. *Organized Complexity*

Order and complexity represent another complementary spatial pairing that evolved because it enhanced human productivity and wellbeing. Complexity signifies a setting rich in detail and diversity, whereas organization is the orderly arrangement of objects in a coherently structured environment.

Complexity signals an environment of ample resources and opportunities. Uniform and featureless spaces, by contrast, typically lack options and are often experienced as monotonous and boring. But exceedingly complex environments often foster confusion and even chaos. Complexity can be made more accessible and understandable by imposing order and organization.

Figure 3.40. The Beijing National Stadium or "Bird's Nest," designed by Jacques Herzog and Pierre de Meuron, was originally used for the 2008 Olympics. The structure's organic shape resulted in its nickname, and its biomimetic design assists in the building's heating and cooling. Despite its organic appearance, the building lacks many biophilic features, appearing more like a sculptural object than an integrated design intended to satisfy the inherent human affinity for nature and to connect people with the culture and ecology of its surrounding space.

Figure 3.41. The Supertree Grove in Gardens by the Bay Park in Singapore, designed by Grant Architects and Wilkinson Eyre Architects, has become a symbol of this urban nation-state's desire to be known as the "City in the Garden." The popularity of the Supertrees reflects their organic shape and biomimetic ability to generate solar energy. Still, the isolated occurrence and artificiality of the trees results in a limited biophilic effect.

Figure 3.42. The Hill Restaurant in the Jardines de Mexico complex near Cuernavaca, Mexico, designed by Vo Trong Nghia, possesses several biophilic features that contribute to its attractiveness. These include prospect and refuge, the use of bamboo and other natural materials, openness to the outside environment, natural geometries, and a feeling of connection to place.

Some of our most successful building and landscape designs possess prominent elements of both organization and complexity. These include such celebrated structures as great religious architecture, castles, and even entire neighborhoods and constructed landscapes in Europe and Asia.

These buildings contain extraordinary detail and diversity, yet offer experiences that are visually coherent and balanced. Much of modern architecture, by contrast, is excessively uniform, homogeneous, and monotonous. Although efficient, these structures often inspire little emotional attachment. This deficiency has sometimes encouraged the designs of buildings that are so detailed and complex that they become unsettling and disorienting. The objective of biophilic design is to create structures that are rich in detail and diversity, yet are experienced in an orderly and meaningful way.

The organic yet organized detail of the masterful Gloucester Cathedral, the multifaceted coherence of a lovely Asian carpet, and the many Gothic details of a university gated stone entryway are all excellent examples of organized complexity (Figures 3.43, 3.44, 3.45).

22. *Mobility*

Mobility is moving with relative effectiveness and efficiency from one spatial environment to another. The absence of clear pathways within and between spaces by contrast often fosters frustration and anxiety; for example, some modern interior building designs favor large open spaces that lack clear boundaries, entry areas, corridors, or exits.

In exterior settings, walks, pathways, and roads often facilitate mobility. Within building interiors, people often navigate from one area to another by relying on corridors, stairs, doors, elevators, escalators, and other spatial connectors. Actual and symbolic links to nature are often used to embellish or inform modes of conveyance within interior settings because these natural features can foster greater comfort and satisfaction.

Figure 3.43. The Gloucester Cathedral in Gloucester, England, exemplifies the biophilic origins of many sacred buildings. Notable features include a vaulted and spacious main hall, treelike supporting columns, a canopy ceiling, natural materials, colored glass windows, areas of prospect and refuge, organic shapes and forms, information richness, and organized complexity.

Figure 3.44. Images and designs inspired by natural forms are often extensively employed in traditional Asian carpets, and are integral to their aesthetic appeal. The biophilic features in this carpet include organic forms, natural materials, natural colors, information richness, and organized complexity.

Figure 3.45. The ornate gateway of a Yale University residential college exemplifies how complexity can still exhibit coherence and orderliness.

For example, a hallway or high glass elevator can employ partitions, images of nature, and natural materials to foster feelings of relation to nature within largely built environments.

Effective biophilic design typically provides clear pathways between spaces and a relative ease of movement between settings such as facilitated by the elegant Ekouin Nenbutsudo Temple in Tokyo, or the magnificent organic-like staircase of the Hotel Bristol Palace in Genoa, Italy (Figures 3.46, 3.47).

23. *Transitional Spaces*

Transitional spaces primarily link the interior of buildings to exterior settings, although they can also connect interior spaces. These transitional areas contribute to people's feelings of orientation, mobility, and security—for without discernible connections between the outside and inside of a building, or between interior spaces, people often experience frustration and a sense of inefficiency. Biophilic transitional spaces often facilitate adaptive shifts from one condition to another; in particular, by creating links to the exterior environment, transitional spaces can generate considerable emotional and aesthetic appeal.

Strategies for encouraging inside-outside connections frequently include porches, patios, balconies, courtyards, pavilions, and gardens. Within building interiors, these transitional spaces can include entry areas, foyers, hallways, and atria.

A powerful transitional link between the inside and outside environment is the attractive stone, wood, and light-filled vestibule at Lyndhurst Mansion in Tarrytown, New York, and the "Floating House" in Punta Arenas, Costa Rica (Figures 3.48, 3.49).

24. *Place*

When people talk about "a sense of place," they are often referring to an emotional attachment they feel for particular settings and environments. This attachment generally

Figure 3.46. Ekouin Nenbutsudo Temple in Tokyo, designed by Yutaka Kawahara Studio, fosters tranquility, calm, and beauty in an urban setting. Several biophilic features contribute to this peaceful effect, including extensive vegetation, transitional connections between the inside and outside environments, natural lighting, and natural materials.

Figure 3.47. The Hotel Bristol Palace staircase in Genoa, Italy, mimics the organic qualities of a mollusk shell. Filtered natural lighting, natural geometries, naturalistic colors, and organic forms further enhance this biophilic effect.

Figure 3.48. This transitional setting at the Lyndhurst Mansion in Tarrytown, New York, designed by Ferdinand Mangold, provides a strong sense of connection between the inside and outside environments. Its biophilic appeal is additionally fostered by qualities of prospect and refuge, natural geometries, natural colors, and natural materials.

Figure 3.49. The Floating House in Punta Arenas, Costa Rica, designed by Benjamin Garcia Saxe, seems to rise above the jungle canopy. Its vantage point provides distant views of the ocean and a strong feeling of connection to nature. The biophilic effect of the house is further enhanced by its natural materials and transitional spaces connecting the inside and outside environments.

includes both social and physical dimensions: with the social comes a cultural and historical emphasis, whereas the physical involves a largely geographical and ecological focus. This special affinity for places is thought to have originated at a point in our species' evolution when control over territories greatly facilitated access to resources, mobility, safety, and sustenance. Even in our modern, highly mobile age, humans covet places where they feel particularly attached, connected, and at home. These settings contribute to feelings of familiarity, comfort, and allegiance.

The emotional attachment to place typically includes a social dimension that emphasizes cultural and historical affinities for others. When shared with others, this feeling often fosters a sense of group identity, shared values, and feelings of community membership, all of which add meaning to people's lives. This cultural attachment to place is often reinforced by particular historic and heroic events that seemingly distinguish a particular group from others.

A sense of place also frequently includes a physical dimension that stresses geographic and ecological factors. Geographic features usually include prominent landmarks, landscapes, geological forms, prevailing weather patterns, and an area's characteristic fauna and flora. People also recognize in the presence of certain ecological systems—mountains, valleys, water bodies, forests, wetlands—aspects of their environment that distinguish it from other places. Some of our most celebrated cities and regions, for example, possess prominent landscape and geological features that drew people to settle there and often continue to distinguish these areas as unique.

Unfortunately, a profound sense of loss of connection—what has been called a growing "placelessness"—has become an affliction of modern life. Many communities have lost their distinctive cultural and geographical character. This effect has been further fostered by the spread of anonymous and featureless design elements in many large-scale retail shopping malls, office complexes, schools, manufacturing facilities, and more. This impoverishment of place has eroded personal and collective identities, community pride, and the sustainability of many areas. The social geographer Edward Relph (1976) has described the problem of placelessness in this way: "If places are . . . a fundamental aspect . . . of security and identity then it is important that the means of experiencing, creating, and maintaining significant places are not lost. There are signs that these very means are disappearing and that 'placelessness'—the weakening of distinct and diverse experiences and identities of place—is now a dominant force. Such a trend marks a major shift in the geographical bases of existence from a deep association with places to rootlessness" (p. 6).

A sense of place is a fundamental biophilic design objective and a goal of sustainable development. When people identify with place, they are more likely to be good stewards and retain these settings over time. Many of our most successful buildings, institutions, and communities elicit strong and enduring attachments to place.

A highly moving interplay of water and landscape in Florence, Italy, and the attempt to sustain the coherence of a semi-planned community in England's Cotswolds region represent traditional and modern examples of seeking a connection to place (Figures 3.50, 3.51).

25. *Integrating Parts to Create Wholes*

The biophilic design concept of "connecting parts to wholes" describes the process of creating connections between various characteristics of a space in order to comprise a coherent ecological experience. Effective biophilic design strives to integrate features of settings and spaces. The effect is often a sequential linking of spaces that includes clear boundaries, a plan for ideal patterns of movement, and an overall identity. Good habitats for people are ecosystems of interrelated parts. This integration of parts to an overall whole fosters human physical and mental health, wellbeing, and productivity.

When elements of a space are inadequately connected to their overall setting, the

Figure 3.50. Florence is famous for its powerful landscape features despite having a metropolitan area population of approximately 1.5 million. Prominent biophilic features contributing to this sense of connection between the built and natural environments include the complementary relationship of land and water, extensive organic shapes and forms, naturalistic colors and textures, information richness, organized complexity, and a strong sense of place.

Figure 3.51. A challenge of modern large-scale residential development is creating a feeling of connection to place in a planned community constructed in a relatively short period of time. This planned community in the Cotswolds, England, a region known for a strong sense of place, attempts to establish this effect by incorporating several biophilic design elements, including the widespread use of natural materials and insertion of features of the local natural environment and the area's cultural traditions.

Figure 3.52. Marcus Beach, a residential development in Noosa, Australia, designed by Bark Design Architects, employs various biophilic features to enrich its appeal. These include prominent inside-outside connections, transitional spaces, and the use of natural materials.

Figure 3.53. This manor house courtyard in the Cotswolds region of England contains many biophilic features that elucidate its attraction and appeal. These include the widespread occurrence of natural materials, organic shapes and forms, and the complementary connection of plants and human-made stone facades. Despite the many details, the overall effect is connected and coherent, resulting in a calming and tranquil setting.

consequence is often a fragmented and disconnected ecological environment. Even extraordinary biophilic design features tend to be undermined and diminished when this disconnection occurs. A beautiful green wall, a lovely landscape painting, even a powerful organic shape are often marginalized and of limited benefit if they are not connected to an overall ecological space.

The Marcus Beach residential development in Australia and the Cotswolds Region manor house represent aesthetically and ecologically ambitious ways to use stone, metal, slate, vegetation, and curved spaces to create a compelling ecological system by integrating parts to create a whole (Figures 3.52, 3.53).

These three elements and twenty-five attributes of considerable significance involved in the practice of biophilic design provide a menu of possibilities for the designer seeking to incorporate the human affinity for nature into the design of a built environment. When applied in an appropriate and tailored fashion, and not as an indiscriminately applied checklist, these options offer a designer a wealth of strategies for applying biophilic design in a thoughtful and effective manner.

FOUR

Biophilic Design Applications

Striking examples of biophilic design could easily fill a large book. Here I provide only a brief review of notable examples over the years, but especially in recent times, as well as an overview of some lessons we might learn from these applications. Both historic and contemporary instances of biophilic design will be showcased, rather than presenting in-depth case studies of current projects. In selecting only a few applications to discuss in this chapter, many outstanding examples of the application of biophilic design will necessarily be omitted. The examples included here are not meant as a judgment on the worthiness or particular relevance of various applications. The choices are often simply a function of my awareness, background, and preferences.

A BRIEF HISTORIC PERSPECTIVE

Why are so many of our most compelling, attractive, and moving examples of biophilic design historic—including many celebrated civic, educational, military, religious, commercial, and hospitality structures? Moreover, why do many historic biophilic applications extend across entire cities such as Kyoto, Venice, Paris, Rome, London, New York, and San Francisco, or regions such as Tuscany, Provence, the Cotswolds, and areas of south Asia? These communities all draw great numbers of admirers and visitors who marvel at the striking loveliness and appeal of their buildings and landscapes.

Many of the constructions in these communities owe much of their special attraction to the various direct and indirect ways that nature is incorporated into them and experienced by their inhabitants. Prominent biophilic features in these built environments often include the widespread use of natural materials, naturalistic images, organic shapes and forms, natural geometries, natural lighting, transitional spaces, information richness, areas of prospect and refuge, organized complexity, a patina due to aging over time, cultural and ecological connections to place, and a wealth of other biophilic design features and attributes.

The inclusion of many biophilic design applications in these historic districts perhaps reflects the availability of certain materials and building technologies during a particular era. But although these limitations may have played a role, they fail to explain the many indirect spatial and symbolic expressions of biophilic design in these structures and landscapes.

Perhaps this historic connection to biophilic design is the result of the survival of large-scale constructions such as cathedrals, citadels, and other civic institutions capable of withstanding the withering effects of time. By contrast, the relative absence of biophilic design features in more modest buildings may merely reflect the fact that many of these attributes have eroded or even disappeared over time. Yet for both monumental and modestly built structures, a major reason given for retaining and restoring them is to preserve a strong connection to nature that they continue to provide. That is, historic biophilic features are frequently cited as the primary reason for sustaining them in today's increasingly non-historic world.

This assertion of the historic importance of biophilic design is not meant to romanticize the past. It would be exceedingly difficult to return to previous historic eras given our modern reliance on manufactured products, advanced technology, and rapid and large-scale construction. Still, we can learn from the past and be guided and inspired by its accomplishments. Many contemporary designs could more fully recognize the success and appeal of those modern structures that manage to both incorporate elements of the natural world and include the historic features of much traditional architecture. We can't replicate the past, but we can seek to selectively "go back to the future" by using the distinctive uses and technologies of our age to capture the best elements of historic biophilic design.

Historic examples of biophilic design can be as widely varied as their geographic locales. Consider the integration of natural imagery, vegetation, water, stone, sense of place, and a serene sense of spirituality at the Shunkoin Temple in Kyoto, Japan, a covered bridge and falls in Bath, England, and the Church of Mary Magdalene in Jerusalem, Israel (Figures 4.1, 4.2, 4.3).

FRANK LLOYD WRIGHT: FROM HISTORIC TO MODERN

The twentieth-century architect Frank Lloyd Wright was distinctive for recognizing the critical role of nature in building design. His fundamental biophilic architectural philosophy was embodied in his iconic quotation, "Study nature, love nature, stay close to nature. It will never fail you." Wright's work marks the transition from historic instances of biophilic design to a more modern application. Yet despite Wright's retrospectively acknowledged greatness, during his lifetime he was often marginalized by his peers. His contemporaries often complained that his unmitigated embrace of the natural world as the exclusive model for design was excessively romantic; it ran counter to the prevailing tenets of modern international architecture, whose focus was one of universal application and a lack of distinctiveness.

Compounding the acceptance of Wright were his often obscure views and method-

Figure 4.1. Shunkoin Temple in Kyoto, Japan, has a serene and spiritual effect on visitors. Various biophilic features contributing to this effect include the widespread use of natural materials, natural geometries, organic shapes and forms, information richness, organized complexity, and areas of prospect and refuge.

Figure 4.2. This traditional scene of a covered bridge and waterfall in Bath, England, includes a historic covered bridge with shops, river and associated spillway, and adjacent neighborhood. The integration of commercial activity, transportation, a residential community, and an energy source is a characteristic of much historic biophilic design, and results in not only many practical benefits but also strong feelings of connection to the culture and ecology of the area.

Figure 4.3. The Church of Mary Magdalene, a Russian Orthodox Church outside Jerusalem, contains several notable biophilic features that contribute to its enduring popularity. These include its onion-shaped domes, natural materials, natural geometries, organized complexity, information richness, and organic forms.

ologies. He worked more by intuition than by using a systematic and standard approach. His work was difficult to emulate because it lacked a clear understanding of human evolution and biology, or a theoretical methodology for incorporating biophilia into the design of the built environment.

Still, his accomplishments were legendary and inspiring. Particularly notable were the residences Fallingwater, Taliesin East and West, and the Prairie houses, as well as larger constructions such as the Johnson Wax Office Building, New York's Guggenheim Museum, and the Marin County Civic Center.

Fallingwater, which was originally constructed as a vacation house some ninety minutes south of Pittsburgh, Pennsylvania, is probably Wright's most recognized design (Figure 4.4). Despite its rural location, the structure annually attracts more than a hundred thousand visitors per year, many of whom view their visit as an architectural pilgrimage. How do we explain Fallingwater's extraordinary appeal? Its most prominent features are its location astride a stream and its seemingly embedded waterfalls that appear to flow in and out of the structure. This dramatic effect is magnified by the residence's close proximity to the falls, rather than being located downstream where this geological feature might be more readily viewed and admired. As the architectural critic Grant Hildebrand insightfully notes, the waterfall's current location makes the occupants feel like participants in, rather than mere spectators of, nature.

Fallingwater embraces a wealth of other biophilic design features that help elucidate its extraordinary appeal and popularity. These include the widespread use of natural materials, natural colors and textures, organic shapes and forms, various points of prospect and refuge, transitional spaces such as decks and porches, the integration of the structure into its geological surroundings, ample hearth-like settings and fireplaces, and organized complexity. Moreover the structure integrates these many distinct details into a larger whole.

Figure 4.4. Fallingwater, a residence located in Mill Run, Pennsylvania, south of Pittsburgh, was designed by Frank Lloyd Wright. Among the many biophilic features that contribute to its extraordinary allure and appeal are a dramatic connection of the house to a nearby stream and waterfalls, the relationship of the structure to its landscape, the extensive use of natural materials, and various areas of prospect and refuge.

Not surprisingly, the design of Fallingwater speaks to a wide range of biophilic values, all of which reinforce its enduring appeal. These include pronounced aesthetic and emotional connections to the natural world and the deliberate attempt to exploit and master one's environment. The building is also a remarkable intellectual and technical accomplishment that inspires elements of fear, awe, and even spiritual reverence stemming from its exaggerated cantilevered projection high over the rocks and waterfalls below.

Finally, the Johnson Wax Office Building in Racine, Wisconsin, is an office structure whose disc-like shapes above and open savannah-like plains below offer a powerful analog of nature incorporated into the design of the built environment (Figure 4.5).

Wright used *organic architecture* to describe his philosophy of nature as a model for architectural design. In fact, he probably coined the term, which has experienced a significant resurgence in recent years. Organic architecture and the somewhat related concept of biomorphic architecture are often used to describe buildings that resemble living organisms, even when these organic shapes do not themselves occur in the natural world.

Prominent examples of organic or biomorphic architecture include the Sydney Opera House, designed by Jørn Utzon, with its "wings" that intimate a bird or a bird of paradise plant; the TWA terminal at New York's JFK airport, designed by Eero Saarinen, which also is evocative of bird wings; and Wright's Guggenheim Museum in New York City, which is designed to suggest the spiraling of a shell. Although all these examples seem lifelike, their forms have no empirical counterparts. These shapes are instead inspired by an understanding of natural forms, and based on principles of organic growth and development.

A remarkable revival of organic architecture appears to have occurred, starting in the later twentieth century. This resurgence is especially apparent in the work of such eminent architects as Frank Gehry, Zaha Hadid, and Santiago Calatrava, as well as some of the designs of Renzo Piano, Norman Foster, and others. The revival of organic architecture is a

Figure 4.5. The Johnson Wax Office Building in Racine, Wisconsin, designed by Frank Lloyd Wright in 1936, is a well-liked and long-used building. Several biophilic features contribute to its positive effect, particularly the central interior space, which has been likened to a savannah landscape with a spreading tree canopy, or a pond with lily pads. Other notable biophilic features include the structure's organic shape, sense of spaciousness, and diffuse natural lighting.

welcome contrast to the sterility of many contemporary built environments, and signifies a renewed admiration for the natural world as a model for design.

Simultaneously, however, modern architecture continues to foster an increasing separation from nature. Reasons for this growing disconnect from the natural world are many and include a reliance on engineering and technology that reinforces a view of nature as superfluous and irrelevant, a preference for straight-line geometries, and an outright rejection of nature as a model for architecture. For many, nature is still very much a resource to be transformed, or a dispensable aesthetic and recreational amenity.

Many examples of "organic architecture" also fall short of the biophilic design ideal. The sinuous curves of Fariborz Sahba's Lotus Temple in New Delhi, India, Hadid's Heydar Aliyev Center in Baku, Azerbaijan, and the remarkable natural geometries of Gehry's Guggenheim Bilbao Museum all admirably evoke impressions of organic life (Figures 4.6, 4.7, 4.8). Yet these structures often lack critical biophilic features, especially in their building interiors. These organic designs seem to stand apart, acting more like sculptural objects rather than habitats where humans live in close connection with the natural world. The aesthetically compelling structures also appear unrelated to the cultural and ecological characteristics of their place. Consequently, many of them seem more like decorative than transformative structures, offering little more than aesthetic appeal to those visitors seeking a deeper relationship to nature.

The contrast between organic and biophilic design is illustrated by two prominent railway centers in New York City—Grand Central Terminal in midtown Manhattan, originally designed in 1871 by John B. Snook, and the recently completed Oculus railway hub in lower Manhattan, designed by Santiago Calatrava (Figures 4.9, 4.10).

The Oculus offers the impression of bird's wings poised for flight. But beyond its organic appearance, the Oculus provides little sense of connection to nature with associated biophilic design features. The building seems to serve as primarily a passageway

Figure 4.6. The Lotus Temple, a Bahá'í House of worship in New Delhi, India, designed by Fariborz Sahba, imitates the shape of a lotus flower. Its admirable organic form is marred by the paucity of other direct or indirect connections to nature, which results in the structure being more symbolic than personally relevant to people's lives.

Figure 4.7. The Heydar Aliyev Center in Baku, Azerbaijan, is another striking example of contemporary organic design. Designer Zaha Hadid's signature style of fluid, curved surfaces creates the sense of a living creature. Despite the building's strong aesthetic appeal, however, the relative absence of other biophilic features results in a largely sequestered and isolated effect.

Figure 4.8. The Guggenheim Museum in Bilbao, Spain, designed by Frank Gehry, has received considerable attention as an example of contemporary organic design. The shape of the building was apparently inspired by the form and texture of a fish, its curved surface further evoking the sense of living nature. Yet the building, which offers few biophilic features beyond its organic form, seems isolated and sculptural rather than well integrated into the culture and ecology of its location.

Figure 4.9. Despite being largely devoid of direct experiences of nature, Grand Central Terminal owes much of its extraordinary appeal to its many biophilic features. Some of its indirect and spatial biophilic attributes include a spacious vault with a nighttime ceiling sky above, widespread use of natural materials, extensive organic shapes and forms, diffuse natural lighting, and areas of prospect and refuge.

Figure 4.10. The recently completed World Trade Center Rail Transportation Hub, or Oculus, in New York City, was designed by Santiago Calatrava. Its form resembles the wings of a bird poised for flight, while the interior space offers a great soaring volume. The structure's shape celebrates life in the face of the terrible death and destruction associated with the September 11, 2001, terrorist attack. Yet beyond its organic shape it includes few biophilic features, which means that it offers little benefit beyond its narrow transportation objective.

rather than as a habitat that can facilitate an enriching human relationship to nature and place.

By contrast, despite few direct connections to nature (hardly a living plant encountered), Grand Central Terminal possesses a wide array of biophilic features that account for its powerful appeal. These include the extensive use of natural materials, shapes, and forms; widespread and diffuse natural lighting; many prospect and refuge as well as transitional spaces; natural colors and textures; information richness; organized complexity; and a compelling ecological integrity and wholeness. Grand Central Terminal, as a consequence, becomes a destination in itself, a place of extensive commercial and social activity where users and visitors alike experience various emotional, intellectual, and even spiritual connections to the natural world.

The revival of organic architecture is a welcome development that signifies a renewed respect and appreciation for nature. By itself, however, it remains an insufficiently comprehensive approach to biophilic design.

LIVING ARCHITECTURE

The term *living architecture* often designates an extensive insertion of living organisms, particularly plants, into the modern built environment. It represents another shift during the past half century toward bringing nature into contemporary building design, a trend in which new technologies facilitate the installation of plants and other living organisms, especially on building facades and interior walls. The deliberate attachment of plant life to buildings (sometimes called facade greening), has been a relatively well-established feature of historic architecture. What makes modern living architecture distinctive is the ambitious scale and scope of these new applications of plant biology and the techniques for managing soil, water, humidity, and other biophysical factors to assure their maintenance and survival.

Much of modern living architecture focuses on the creation of green roofs and green walls, and extensive plantings within atria and courtyards. Practitioners associated with the growth of living architecture include Steven Peck, who is known for his promotion of green roofs, and Patrick Blanc, who is famous for creating elaborate green walls. Green roofs can accomplish many low-environmental-impact objectives such as storm water capture and occasional reuse, energy insulation, reduced levels of carbon dioxide and other air pollutants, and the enhancement of biodiversity. Green roofs can also help city planners and others achieve many biophilic design objectives in otherwise barren, featureless buildings, such as increasing people's exposure to nature in city settings, offering more opportunities for rest and the appreciation of natural beauty in largely urban park-like settings, and providing a habitat for a variety of living creatures.

These examples of living architecture represent admirable strategies for connecting people with nature in the modern built environment, and so for improving their health, productivity, and wellbeing. Yet much of living architecture falls short of being an ideal approach to biophilic design, especially when it appears to be an isolated feature of a building or landscape that is otherwise dominated by nonbiophilic design features. The implementation of green roofs and vertical plant walls can add vitality, color, and other compelling biophilic attributes to a building. But to achieve its full potential, and avoid becoming merely a high-maintenance curiosity, living architecture must connect to other design features within an integrated ecological biophilic whole. By itself, it remains an insufficient basis for a truly transformative application of biophilic design.

Living architecture can be powerfully revealed at a variety of scales. A single green wall, like that encountered in the Diesel Corporation's headquarters in Vicenza, Italy, brings a natural feel to its immediate environment (Figure 4.11).

Figure 4.11. The Diesel Corporation, an Italian retail clothing company, constructed new headquarters in 2010 in Vicenza, Italy. The interior, designed by Studio Ricatti, includes a large vertical "green" plant wall. The building contains other biophilic features such as widespread natural lighting, natural materials, and water elements. The overall impact is positive, although a lack of integration of these various biophilic features within the building's overall design results in a somewhat discordant effect.

On a larger scale, the Park Royal Hotel in Singapore and the Bosco Verticale residential complex in Milan provide two powerful examples of how living architecture can transform a building's entire exterior design (Figures 4.12, 4.13).

BUILDING TYPES

For much of the twentieth century, building and landscape design has favored a narrow engineering and technological approach to construction. The result has largely been barren, featureless structures that mostly ignore the human need for contact with nature. Periodic attempts to fundamentally alter this perspective of building design can be seen in such architectural design movements as art nouveau, arts and crafts, vernacular, and organic architecture. These efforts are important precursors of biophilic design. They lack, however, a basic understanding of the role of nature in human evolution and biology, and a related systematic framework for incorporating natural patterns and processes into the design of the built environment.

Many outstanding examples of biophilic design are nonetheless evident in various buildings and landscapes. These notable precedents cover a wide variety of building uses, especially people's residences, where the small scale, personal motivation, and relatively affordable costs often lead to innovative ways of bringing nature into people's everyday lives.

Moreover, many impressive examples of biophilic design are encountered in various uses of building applications and types. These typically cover the fields of healthcare, work, education, retail commerce, residential development, hospitality services, and what has sometimes been called sacred architecture.

Healthcare Facilities

For much of the twentieth century most healthcare facilities discouraged contact with nature, especially in interior settings. Nature was frequently regarded as an indicator of a primitive healthcare system and a significant source of contamination and disease. Conventional hospitals and other healthcare facilities were consequently often featureless, barren settings, artificially lit and ventilated, and dominated by the presence of complex technology.

These assumptions regarding the irrelevancy of nature as therapeutic and healing have shifted significantly during the past half century. The studies cited in Chapter 1 demonstrate that exposure to nature can have significant positive physical and emotional effects, including stress relief, pain mitigation, and even recovery from illness. Furthermore, the positive presence of nature in the healthcare workplace enhances staff morale, improves visitor-staff interactions, and aids in employee recruitment and retention. One example of a waiting room that caused high stress but then was transformed into a peaceful and calming setting can be seen in Figures 4.14 and 4.15. The incorporation of biophilic design principles has also utterly transformed patient rooms. These previously dull, featureless, and artificial spaces are unrecognizable after their redesign, with patients, visitors, and healthcare staff enjoying the positive effects of vegetation, natural materials, and powerful presentations of nature (Figures 4.16, 4.17).

Examples of healthcare institutions that have successfully applied biophilic principles include Khoo Teck Puat Hospital in Singapore and Smilow Cancer Center at Yale-New Haven Hospital in New Haven, Connecticut. Khoo Teck Puat Hospital includes an astonishing array of terrestrial and aquatic plants and animals in a mainly exterior environment that also features flowing water in streams, waterfalls, and nearby lakes. The facility proudly records and photographs its butterflies, birds, fish, and other wildlife. And con-

Figure 4.12. The Park Royal Hotel in the Pickering area of Singapore, designed by WOHA Architects, has become a model of how to incorporate living nature into a vertical building space. The building's widespread exterior plantings at multiple levels contribute to its claim of being a hotel-as-garden. Additional biophilic features include cantilevered sky gardens, extensive interior vegetation, natural materials, and water features.

Figure 4.13. "Bosco Verticale" is a residential complex consisting of two towers in Milan designed by Boeri Studio. This residential development is distinctive for using trees in its building exterior to create a sense of connection to nature in a highly urban setting.

Figures 4.14 and 4.15. A windowless and featureless waiting room prior to its renovation resulted in high levels of stress and aggressive behavior among visitors, patients, and staff. The renovation to the same windowless space incorporated several biophilic features to create a more positive and calming effect. These included a large and colorful mural of a savannah, natural material furnishings, and plants. Research by Roger Ulrich (2008) and colleagues demonstrated that significant reductions in stress and conflict occurred following the renovation.

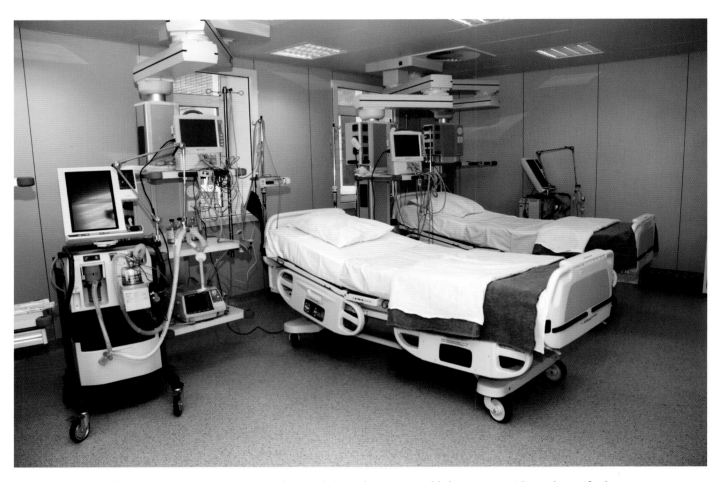

Figures 4.16 and 4.17. Many hospital rooms lack windows or natural lighting, extensively employ artificial materials, and are dominated by the appearance of highly technological equipment. Research has revealed that these often-barren settings foster stress and anxiety. By contrast, hospital rooms that incorporate such biophilic features as natural lighting, natural materials, images of nature, and outside views have been found to enhance patient, visitor, and staff comfort and satisfaction, and to create a more therapeutic environment.

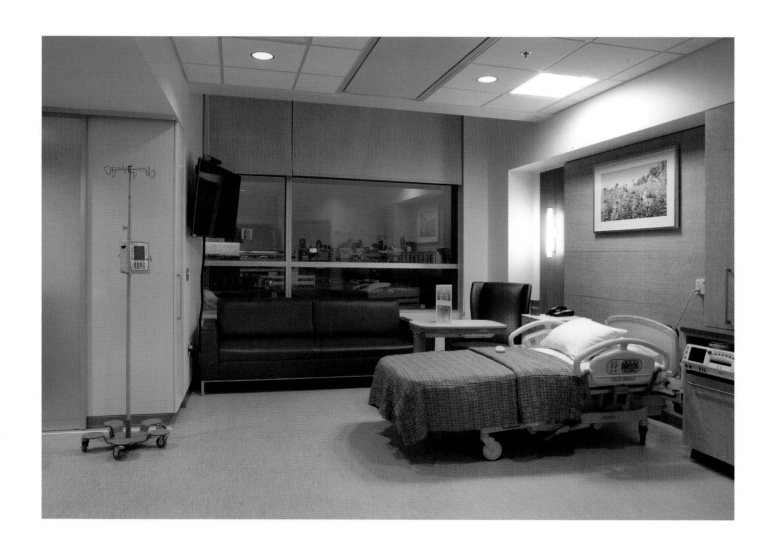

tact with domesticated nature is encouraged in a rooftop garden where cultivated vegetables, herbs, and other crops are grown, not by patients, but typically by elderly nearby residents who have built ties between the hospital and its neighboring community. For all these reasons, Khoo Teck Puat Hospital truly reflects Singapore's goal of being the "City in the Garden" (Figure 4.18).

The Smilow Cancer Center at Yale-New Haven Hospital has largely reversed this interior-exterior equation (Figure 4.19). Its external environment still consists of a featureless building facade, impervious street and parking surfaces, and little vegetative cover except for its lovely healing garden. By contrast, the building's interior, largely designed by Roz Cama, includes extensive occurrences of direct and indirect contact with nature. For example, the entry area is a naturally lit atrium filled with plants, as well as the sight and sound of water. Throughout the building is an extraordinary array of high-quality and thematically organized artworks consisting of landscapes, plants, and animals—as well as furnishings, fabrics, and sidings largely consisting of natural materials. Live tropical fish tanks and a healing garden, which includes a prominent water feature, provide more direct exposure to nature.

Buildings for Work

Office space and manufacturing plants for much of the nineteenth and twentieth centuries viewed contact with nature as largely a waste of money, space, and time. The efficient use of space was seen as a central challenge, one that could be overcome with the use of advanced technology. Consequently many work settings were largely sensory-deprived, artificially lit, windowless spaces. The typical factory and office worker toiled in a mainly barren environment far removed from features of the natural world. These impoverished settings were even likened to the cages of the old-style zoo, which was ironically eventually banned as inhumane for zoo animals. These work settings had somehow become acceptable for people as not really biological creatures with analogous ecological needs (Figure 4.20).

Multiple factors contributed to the alienation from nature that characterized many office and manufacturing settings. Particularly significant were cost-benefit analyses that favored short-term calculations of technological efficiencies and the desire to show off recent advances in engineering, which ignored long-term health effects. From this perspective, economic success was regarded as mainly the product of science and technology, whereas contact with nature was a largely trivial sign of backwardness. Advances in construction materials, such as modern glass, further allowed for the widespread construction of largely airtight buildings with significant proportions of windowless space (Figures 4.21, 4.22).

These attitudes have been slowly shifting during the past quarter century, spurred by empirical and anecdotal research that has found that connections with nature often contribute to worker satisfaction, health, performance, recruitment, and retention. Examples include the Genzyme office building in Cambridge, Massachusetts, designed by Stefan Behnisch Architects; the Herman Miller factory and office complex in Holland, Michigan, designed by William McDonnough; and the new World Wildlife Fund Centre outside London, designed by Michael Hopkins Architects.

The Genzyme Corporation is a leading biotechnology company that constructed a new headquarters in 2005. The exterior of the building seems quite conventional—a rectangular structure surrounded by a largely environmentally degraded landscape. The building interior, however, has several notable and innovative biophilic features. The great central atrium, for example, is a naturally lit space that includes, from the ground floor to the skylight rooftop above, a wide diversity of plants, small park-like settings, and a water feature. The atrium's extraordinary natural lighting is achieved by a remarkable design feature involving a complex system of reflective mirrors. Rooftop heliostat mirrors track

Figure 4.18. Khoo Teck Puat Hospital in Singapore refers to itself as a "hospital in a garden." The exterior setting includes an extraordinary quantity and diversity of tropical plants, butterfly and bird species, and several prominent water features. This melding of nature and the built environment offers patients, visitors, and staff an attractive, calming, and therapeutic setting. It has also drawn the interest and support of the nearby neighbors, who use the rooftop garden to grow fruits and vegetables.

Figure 4.19. The healing garden at Smilow Cancer Center, a unit of Yale-New Haven Hospital in New Haven, Connecticut, is a nature-oriented area in an urban hospital that has enhanced morale and relieved stress for patients, visitors, and staff.

Figure 4.20. The average office worker in the United States works in a windowless, sensory-deprived setting. These often-barren cubicles have been likened to the cages of an old-style zoo, where animals denied exposure to nature experienced diverse physical and mental health ailments. These traditional zoo cages are now banned as inhumane, despite humans ironically continuing to work under analogous conditions. People in these windowless settings are more likely than others to insert pictures of nature and plants as a way of creating a more biophilic environment.

the sun's movement across the course of the day, reflecting its natural light onto skylight louvers that channel it onto small internal glass mirrors hanging from steel cables at varying heights like a giant mobile. The overall effect is not just highly functional, but also beautiful (see Figure 3.1).

The extensive natural lighting, interior park-like spaces, and widespread vegetation at Genzyme appear to have significantly contributed to a highly appealing and productive work environment. Anecdotal evidence indicates a significant improvement in hours worked, increased employee collaboration (a goal of the new construction), and superior recruitment and retention of highly paid professionals. (For more on how biophilic design addresses these and other objectives, see Chapter 2.)

The Herman Miller factory and office complex (see also Chapter 2) includes such innovative biophilic design features as extensive natural lighting, vegetation, and a restored prairie landscape. As noted in Chapter 2, research conducted by Judith Heerwagen and colleagues revealed nine months after construction a 20 percent increase in worker productivity, a significant decrease in employee absenteeism and symptoms of illness, and a considerable increase in employee feelings of wellbeing.

A more recent example of the benefits of worker exposure to nature occurred in 2012 at the new World Wildlife Fund Centre outside London (Figure 4.23). The client wanted a relatively open floor plan to optimize flexible and adaptable workspace. This type of work environment, however, often leads to processed air, windowless office cubicles reliant on artificial lighting, and a general disconnection from nature. The challenge was addressed by designing a large natural-light-filled cavity consisting of a curved ceiling, oversized windows at either end of the work area, skylights, extensive wood paneling, and abundant mature vegetation extending from the lower floor to the upper workspace.

Figures 4.21 and 4.22. Many glass office towers are designed in the International Style and closely resemble one another regardless of their geographic location, local culture, and ecology. These structures generally contain few biophilic features, relying instead on the widespread use of artificial materials, a rigidly engineered geometry, a lack of organic detail, sealed and nonoperable windows, and homogeneous glass facades. These structures provide few physical and mental benefits for their occupants based on the inherent human affinity for nature. They also often adversely affect nonhuman life, as illustrated by the many birds that die after crashing into the highly transparent and reflective glass.

Figure 4.23. The new World Wildlife Fund Centre outside London, designed by Michael Hopkins Architects, combines the efficiency and flexibility of an open office floor plan with feelings of connection to nature. This has been facilitated by the extensive use of natural lighting, outside views, a curved wooden ceiling, skylights, and abundant and mature vegetation.

Built Environments for Education

Historically, many educational facilities have underestimated the value of contact with nature. The prevailing pedagogy treated learning as a largely indoor, abstract, non-experiential process. Contact with nature was mainly regarded as a recreational break from serious learning, or the mark of a primitive educational system. Even outdoor play was largely confined to artificial equipment and surfaces.

These practices have slowly changed in response to research that has identified benefits stemming from contact with nature. Research has shown that students exposed to natural lighting, plants, and a more nature-oriented curriculum have higher test scores, improved motivation, and better health. Schools with enhanced natural features such as Yale University's Gothic-style campus also have better teacher and staff morale, recruitment, and retention (Figure 4.24).

The renovated Sidwell Friends Middle School in Washington, D.C., designed by KieranTimberlake, and Kroon Hall, a relatively new facility of the Yale University School of Forestry and Environmental Studies, designed by Michael Hopkins Architects, are two examples of the shift to more biophilically designed schools (Figures 4.25, 4.26).

The Sidwell Friends Middle School renovation transformed a conventional 1950s building with few sustainable and biophilic design features into one with many enhanced connections to nature. For example, the previous building relied largely on artificial lighting and materials, featured relatively small windows that inhibited visual access to the outside, and had an impervious surrounding landscape. By contrast, the renovated facility includes biophilic features such as extensive natural and reclaimed materials, large windows, widespread natural lighting and ventilation, a green roof and rainwater capture system, enhanced energy efficiency, and an ecologically restored entry area.

The entry area was converted from an existing hard artificial surface into an evocative

Figure 4.24. The Gothic style architecture of various residential, teaching, and library buildings at Yale University, designed by James Gamble Rogers, has several biophilic features that contribute to its enduring appeal. These include the widespread use of natural materials, shapes and forms inspired by nature, transitional spaces such as courtyards, areas of prospect and refuge, a strong sense of place, information richness, and organized complexity.

Figure 4.25. The Sidwell Friends Middle School renovation in Washington, D.C., by KieranTimberlake Architects, transformed an anonymous structure into a stimulating and appealing building. Biophilic features contributing to this effect include the widespread use of natural materials, natural lighting, rain gardens, a green roof, and especially the conversion of a previous hard-surface entry into a wetlands that treats the building's storm and gray water and has been incorporated into the school curriculum.

Figure 4.26. Kroon Hall, the administrative and teaching building of the Yale University School of Forestry and Environmental Studies in New Haven, Connecticut, was designed by Michael Hopkins Architects and built in 2009. The building contains several biophilic features that account for its widespread popularity. These include the extensive use of natural materials, natural shapes and forms, natural lighting, natural geometries, organized complexity, and a feeling of connection to the culture and history of the site.

and educational fresh water wetland "front door." This terraced wetland not only captures rain that then helps with treatment of the building's gray water; its ecological functioning has also become part of the school's curriculum, and a powerful statement of the school's commitments to environmental stewardship and making nature an essential part of the learning process.

Kroon Hall, the administrative and teaching center of the Yale University School of Forestry and Environmental Studies, was built in 2009 by Michael Hopkins Architects to be a model of low environmental impact and biophilic design. Its unique and admirable features resulted in the building receiving the U. S. Green Building Council's highest platinum LEED (Leadership in Energy and Environmental Design) award.

Kroon Hall's impressive biophilic design attributes include the replacement of a largely impervious landscape with vegetated courtyards, a rainwater garden, a native plant entry area, a stone facade, and many transitional spaces such as courtyards, colonnades, and areas of prospect and refuge. The building's interior, in particular, contains several notable biophilic features such as the extensive use of organic shapes and images; the widespread use of natural materials, especially wood sustainably harvested from the school's nearby forests; extensive natural lighting and natural ventilation; prominent outside views; natural geometries, particularly curved surfaces and fractals; natural textures and colors; information richness; and organized complexity. It has overall an ecologically coherent environment characterized by a strong sense of place.

Just having a low-impact design is not enough. Consider the Bren Graduate School of Environmental Science and Management at the University of California in Santa Barbara, which serves a similar clientele as Kroon Hall. Both facilities received the U.S. Green Building Council's highest platinum rating for their many accomplishments in the realm of low environmental impact. Yet the Bren building includes few biophilic design features—even its Pacific Ocean site is largely dominated by a windowless auditorium, administrative offices, and nonteaching spaces. The difference in the impact on occupants of the two buildings is suggested by their response to these two environments: Kroon Hall elicits strong affection and extensive use, whereas the occupants of Bren report less interest and commitment to this facility.

The new Sandy Hook Elementary School is another notable example of biophilic design (Figure 4.27). The previous building employed a largely traditional school architecture that contained little overt relationship to the natural environment. The new facility, designed by Svigals + Partners and constructed in 2015, with my input, affirms and celebrates life and the connection to nature in ways that honor the schoolchildren and teachers who tragically died there.

Notable biophilic design features include extensive natural lighting, a constructed wetlands, courtyards, shapes and forms inspired by nature, and other nature-rich attributes. The result is a building that enhances the children's learning and living environment while promoting their safety and security.

Shopping Centers and Districts

During the twentieth century box-store shopping malls rose and triumphed, only to hopefully meet their demise in the current era. These shopping centers present featureless, windowless, artificially lit, rectangular buildings that lack sensory stimulation. Surrounded by an impervious parking surface, with little, if any, connection to nature, these temples of commerce are often largely separated from the culture and ecology of their locations and settings—so much so that nearly identical versions occur across the globe (Figure 4.28). The conventional shopping mall is the icon of a kind of least-cost construction and straight-line engineering that treats the experience of nature as largely an irrelevancy. The great commercial shopping districts in cities such as New York, London, and Paris, however, compete well with the shopping mall. Upon close examination, the design

Figure 4.27. The new 2016 Sandy Hook Elementary School in Newtown, Connecticut, designed by Barry Svigals of Svigals + Partners, assisted by the author, incorporated several biophilic design strategies. An objective was to affirm life at this site of incomprehensible tragedy. Biophilic features that contribute to this effect include constructed wetlands, natural swales, courtyards, interior connections to the outside environment, wildlife feeders and gardens, natural materials, a sinuous geometry, natural lighting, and interior images of nature.

Figure 4.28. This typical shopping mall is sterile, lifeless, and unappealing to the senses. Most of the box-like stores lack natural lighting, natural materials, and other connections to nature. The mall largely contains artificial materials, artificial geometries, extensive vehicular access, and an enormous, asphalt parking surface.

of many of these famous urban retail structures reveals many biophilic features that help them to sustain their appeal and distinctiveness.

The popularity of the conventional box-store shopping center largely stemmed from competitive pricing, convenient access and parking, and controlled climatic conditions. Yet the appeal of many malls has waned in recent years, in part because of their oppressive and artificial design.

Ironically, many new and renovated shopping centers are incorporating biophilic design features as a strategy for making these commercial malls more appealing and attractive. These renovated suburban shopping centers have introduced extensive vegetation, natural materials, natural lighting, outdoor amenities, vernacular architecture, pedestrian-only streets, and other biophilic design attributes. It would be an ironic twist of history if these new and renovated shopping center developers became leaders and innovators in adopting biophilic design. If nothing else, it would attest to the power of consumer choice in a capitalist society, despite the irrationalities that exist in a free market system.

Two examples of more biophilically designed shopping areas are the New Seasons Market in Portland, Oregon, and Ülemiste Centre in Tallinn, Estonia. Both prominently include earth-tone colors and vegetation, extensive natural lighting, curved shapes, biophilically designed interface carpeting, and other biophilic design features (Figures 4.29, 4.30).

Homes

Individual residences often contain prominent biophilic design features, perhaps both because the people living there perceive that nature can contribute to the comfort and beauty of one's home, and because it is relatively easy to create or change a home design. When the motivation and resources exist, most people extensively employ natural materials, natural lighting, exterior views, images of nature, fireplaces and hearth-like

Figure 4.29. The courtyard of the New Seasons Market in Portland, Oregon, designed by Alan Jones, provides a powerful inside-outside transitional space that has become esteemed for its beauty and as a place of relaxation. Biophilic design attributes that contribute to this effect include the widespread use of natural materials, a vertical green vegetated wall, and a complex yet orderly and coherent space.

Figure 4.30. The Ülemiste Centre in Tallinn, Estonia, is the largest retail shopping mall in the country with more than two hundred stores. Its largely conventional exterior contains few biophilic features, with the shopping center largely surrounded by impervious parking surface. The shopping mall's interior, however, includes several biophilic features that mitigate this effect, such as extensive natural lighting, curved surfaces, natural colors, and pioneering biophilic design carpeting produced by Interface, Inc.

settings, areas of prospect and refuge, naturalistic planting, and other biophilic design features.

Examples of personal residences that feature especially evocative biophilic designs include the Casa San Sen residence in Valle de Bravo, Mexico, designed by Alejandro Sánchez García, and the "Cluny House" designed by Guz Wilkinson Architects of Singapore (Figures 4.31, 4.32). Each is distinguished by extensive vegetation, connections between the interior and exterior areas, natural materials, natural lighting, and many other biophilic design features.

Planners of large-scale housing developments, however, have typically ignored the virtues and benefits of connecting to nature in the modern built environment (Figure 4.33). These developments instead typically focus on a narrow understanding of efficiency, employing homogeneous and featureless construction, denuding their landscapes, and deferring to the requirements of extensive vehicular parking. Contact with nature is treated mainly as a superfluous cost yielding little tangible benefit. This featureless and often lifeless construction is often described as urban sprawl.

Recent research, however, has begun to demonstrate how contact with nature in and around homes can yield health benefits and improve residents' wellbeing and quality of life, regardless of their socioeconomic background or circumstances. For example, a study of architecturally mediocre public housing in Chicago that primarily serves a very poor and minority population reported that even the simple inclusion of grass and trees greatly contributed to the residents' health and quality of life (Figures 4.34, 4.35; see also Chapter 2).

A housing development known as Village Homes, located near Davis, California, and designed by Judith and Michael Corbett, provides a good middle-income example (Figure 4.36). This residential development, situated on a sixty-acre tract, includes 220 residences that are an average 2,200 square feet each, a small office complex, and a com-

Figure 4.31. The private residence Casa San Sen in Valle de Bravo, Mexico, designed by Alejandro Sánchez García, contains several biophilic features that contribute to its appeal. These include prominent inside-outside connections, the widespread use of natural materials, natural lighting, views of nature, and proximity to relatively undisturbed natural areas.

Figure 4.32. The Cluny residence in Singapore, designed by Guz Wilkinson Architects, incorporates several biophilic design features that contribute to its appeal and attraction. These include green roofs, natural materials, the presence of water, inside-outside transitional spaces, and a strong sense of connection to the area's tropical setting.

Figure 4.33. Featureless residential development leads to unappealing and often unsustainable environments known as urban sprawl. These nonbiophilic settings often rely on artificial materials, artificial geometries, an impoverished landscape, and disconnection from the culture and ecology of place.

Figures 4.34 and 4.35. The simple presence of even limited grass and trees in an architecturally deficient Chicago public housing project resulted in significant emotional, intellectual, and physical benefits when compared with architecturally identical buildings lacking vegetation and surrounded by an impervious surface.

Figure 4.36. Village Homes, designed by Judith and Michael Corbett, is a planned residential community near Davis, California. It contains several biophilic attributes that have contributed to the project's social and financial success. These include extensive shared open space, pedestrian and bicycle paths, the placement of vehicles at the periphery rather than center of the development, naturalistic plantings, natural drainage swales, and a strong feeling of connection to place.

munity center. Individual homeowners chose relatively small lots so that a larger proportion of the development could be devoted to shared open space, which comprises approximately one-quarter of the overall area and includes pedestrian and bike paths, common
agricultural and recreational areas, natural drainage swales, and a greenbelt that encircles
the complex. Village Homes was also designed with relatively narrow streets and parking
areas confined to the periphery of the development.

Anecdotal and empirical evidence suggests several positive economic and quality-of-
life outcomes at Village Homes. Decades following the complex's construction, housing
prices are significantly higher at Village Homes than at comparable developments that
lack its biophilic design features. Showing a greater attachment to place, residents know
on average forty of their neighbors compared with eighteen in a similar nearby development. Parents at Village Homes have especially praised the way its design allows children to play outdoors in a safe, secure, and nature-rich environment. This child-friendly
quality is reflected in the recollections of a young man raised at Village Homes who today
laments the loss of his once-biophilic lifestyle: "Growing up in Village Homes gave me a
sense of freedom and safety that would be difficult to find in the usual urban neighborhood. The orchards … gardens, and greenbelts within Village Homes offered many stimulating, exciting, joyful places for me to play with friends. We could walk out our back
doors into greenbelts full of all kinds of trees to climb with fruit to eat and gardens with
vegetables to nibble on. Even though we were young, the network of green belts allowed
my friends and I to go anywhere in the community without facing the danger of crossing
a street. Now that I am no longer living in Village Homes, I feel locked in by the fence
in my backyard and the street in front of my house. I feel a loss of the freedom I had as
a child" (Corbett and Corbett 2000, p. 21).

Hospitality-Oriented Structures

Hospitality is a term that has been used to describe buildings whose purpose is to provide a temporary home away from home. These built environments range from simple short-term motels to large, famous resorts and hotels. Many of these structures, especially the larger resorts and hotels, contain impressive biophilic features.

Resorts' quest to help guests feel close to nature likely is driven by a desire to create what people dream of for their vacation getaway: an escape from the everyday world to an idyllic setting that includes extensive gardens, flowers, water features, natural materials, natural lighting, spectacular views, and exposure to weather, as well as facades, fixtures, and furnishings inspired by nature. The "Crosswaters" Ecolodge in Longmen, China, designed by Paul Pholeros and Joseph Lalli of EDSA, is a good example of hospitality-focused biophilic design (Figure 4.37).

Yet the hospitality industry also includes buildings with practically little connection to nature. These barren, sensory-deprived, nondescript designs are often surrounded by hard-surface parking. The contemporary strip motel, much like the conventional shopping mall, often seems like a poster child for this kind of artificial, mind-numbing, non-biophilic architecture (Figure 4.38).

Yet even a modest rectangular room can be designed as an appealing and attractive biophilic space. I recently encountered an example in a relatively modest-sized hotel room. Despite the room only having a small window and limited view, it was creatively and aesthetically designed to include several prominent biophilic features that profoundly contributed to its comfort and appeal. These biophilic designs included floral carpeting, curtains, and couch fabrics; widespread use of natural materials, especially wood, wool, cotton, and leather; tasteful landscape paintings and pictures; earth-tone colors; flower-filled vases; organiclike fixtures, masonry, and metalwork; a fireplace and hearth; a high

Figure 4.37. The Crosswaters Ecolodge in Longmen, China, designed by Paul Pholeros and Joseph Lalli of EDSA, includes several biophilic features that contribute to its appeal. These include close proximity to water and surrounding vegetation, natural materials, natural geometries, and a strong sense of place.

Figure 4.38. This typical strip motel possesses little appeal beyond its affordability and convenient parking. Its alienating nonbiophilic features include artificial geometries, artificial materials, anonymous and repetitive design, the dominance of an impervious parking surface, and disconnection from the culture and ecology of its location.

and somewhat curved ceiling; information richness and organized complexity; and an overall ecologically integrated space (Figure 4.39).

Sacred Architecture

Sacred architecture refers to spiritually and often religiously evocative buildings and spaces. These structures typically contain a surprising number of biophilic features, so much so that an argument can be made for biophilic design being a central part of the sacred experience. Indeed, the origin of much sacred architecture appears to be a strong sense of connection to nature and creation.

With a greater emphasis on more indirect and subtle spatial ways, biophilia is often revealed. In the nave of the Sainte-Chapelle in Paris, the Blue Mosque in Istanbul, and the Tōdai-ji Temple's Daibutsuden (Great Buddha Hall) in Nara, Japan, we encounter the widespread occurrence of biophilic design strategies, including the extensive use of natural materials, shapes, and forms that simulate nature; cavernous outdoorlike spaces; treelike columns; diffuse and scattered natural light; areas of prospect and refuge; natural geometries; organized complexity; and information richness (Figures 4.40, 4.41, 4.42). Furthermore, even the most interior spaces of these sacred structures, such as the nave of Sainte-Chapelle, foster a feeling of being transported from the building's interior to its upward reaches, where organically shaped sculpture and windows further facilitate the transition outside into nature.

Unfortunately, many of our contemporary examples of sacred architecture have lost or degraded this connection with nature. A striking exception is the celebrated Thorn-crown Chapel of Eureka Springs, Arkansas, designed by Fay Jones and constructed in 1980 (Figure 4.43). This structure's biophilic qualities are central to its extraordinary appeal and the strong feelings of affection and appreciation it fosters. By contrast, despite its

Figure 4.39. Several biophilic features result in a satisfying and attractive hotel room at the Sherry-Netherland Hotel in New York City, despite its being a relatively simple square space. These include the extensive use of natural materials, the organic designs of fabrics and fixtures, images of nature, operable windows, and plants and flowers.

Figure 4.40. The Gothic nave of the Sainte-Chapelle in Paris remarkably blends natural colors, natural materials, natural light, and shapes and forms inspired by nature. The result is a beautiful and spiritually inspiring space.

Figure 4.41. The Blue Mosque in Istanbul, Turkey, first constructed more than a thousand years ago, owes much of its enduring popularity to the structure's many biophilic features. These include its spacious interior vault, widespread use of natural materials, shapes and forms that evoke nature, and natural geometries.

Figure 4.42. The Buddhist temple Tōdai-ji Daibutsuden in Nara, Japan, contains several biophilic features that contribute to its timeless appeal. These include the widespread use of natural materials, natural geometries, and organic shapes and forms.

Figure 4.43. The biophilic roots of sacred architecture are prominent in many historic examples of religious architecture. A powerful modern version, however, is the Mildred B. Cooper Thorncrown Chapel in Eureka Springs, Arkansas, designed by Fay Jones. Evident biophilic features at Thorncrown include the extensive use of natural materials, natural geometries, shapes and forms inspired by nature, organized complexity, and a strong sense of connection to place.

Figure 4.44. Many modern religious structures share the affliction of most examples of contemporary architecture: they are largely divorced from the natural world. The exterior design of the St. John's University Abbey Church in Collegeville, Minnesota, exemplifies this relative absence of a natural connection.

many admirable qualities, St. John's University Abbey Church in Collegeville, Minnesota, does not create this kind of powerful relationship to nature (Figure 4.44).

BIOPHILIC DESIGN AT THE URBAN OR COMMUNITY SCALE

Biophilic designs can also be implemented across a community or even an entire city. Implementing these design principles across a larger landscape, however, poses unique problems. First, property rights in a free-market society are generally tied to a single structure or small clusters of buildings rather than entire neighborhoods and urban areas, so acquiring the authority to make changes across a large geographic area can be difficult. Second, cities and communities encompass an enormous range of cultural and ecological diversity, making the task of effectively implementing biophilic design at this scale exceedingly challenging. Finally, most urban areas have historically emphasized the dominance and transformation of nature rather than the celebration of the outdoors, and so have often encouraged environmental waste, pollution, and separation from the natural environment. Changing this dominant paradigm of urban development is a far more daunting task than altering the design of a single building or landscape.

Environmental degradation and alienation from nature, however, should not be considered inevitable consequences of urban and community life. As we learned in Chapter 2, a variety of critical physical and mental benefits are associated with people's enhanced exposure to nature in urban areas. The pioneering landscape architect Frederick Law Olmsted offered us a vision more than a century ago of city residents enjoying a beneficial connection with nature: "A man's eyes cannot be as much occupied as they are in large cities by artificial things . . . without a harmful effect, first on his mental and nervous system and ultimately on his entire constitutional organization . . . The charm of natural scenery is an influence of the highest curative value . . . tending, more than any single form of medication we can use, to establish sound minds in sound bodies" (Beveridge and Rocheleau 1995, p. 68).

Although biophilic design at the urban scale is not easily accomplished, it can theoretically at least be woven back into the everyday lives of those who live, work, and play in contemporary urban areas. Consider Florence and Venice, which were designed and built so long ago (Figure 4.45). Significant progress is also being made in Paris, Chicago, Milan, Taipei, and other cities across the globe. The approach being taken to implementing biophilic design at the urban scale is more ambitious although not altogether new. These urban areas have maintained and enhanced significant connections to nature by reimagining existing parks and open spaces, as well as by creating new forms of engagement with natural features in residential neighborhoods. The Biophilic Cities Network (biophiliccities.org) and its main champion, the urban planner Timothy Beatley, have been leading the way in promoting these initiatives.

Chicago and Paris offer potential inspiring examples of historic and contemporary biophilic design at the urban scale. Chicago's City Hall is now capped with a highly vegetated and naturally beautiful green roof (Figure 4.46). In Paris, prominent biophilic elements include the widespread occurrence of natural materials; natural geometries (particularly fractals); organic forms; transitional spaces such as balconies and courtyards; the prominence of the river Seine; diverse yet coherently related buildings and neighborhoods; and more. Modern Paris continues its tradition of innovative associations with nature in the vertical greening projects of Patrick Blanc and the 4.5-mile Promenade Plantée—a linear park that sits astride an old railway line with commercial stores below (Figure 4.47). Its success has been a catalyst for the economic and social revival of its Paris location.

The experiences of Paris, Chicago, Milan, Taipei, and other cities are both instructive and inspiring. Yet the obstacles to creating beneficial connections to nature in the con-

Figure 4.45. The city of Venice is perhaps the most recognized symbol of biophilic design at an urban scale, even if its attributes are largely relevant to a historic age and a unique environmental context. Among the city's most noticeable features are the ubiquitous presence of water and nonvehicular transport. It also features the extensive use of natural materials, organic shapes and forms, natural geometries, areas of prospect and refuge, information richness, organized complexity, and a strong sense of connection to the culture and ecology of its location.

Figure 4.46. The green roof of Chicago's City Hall, designed by Atelier Dreiseitl and Conservation Design Forum, transformed a barren, heat-trapping asphalt roof into an ecologically and aesthetically compelling urban habitat that is attractive to human and nonhuman life alike—though its human impact is limited by the area's restricted access. Low-environmental-impact features include storm water capture, reduced carbon emissions, and increased insulation. The rooftop also highlights the biophilic design elements of extensive natural vegetation, color, and beauty.

Figure 4.47. Promenade Plantée, constructed on an old rail line in East Paris, and designed by Jacques Vergely and Phillippe Mathieux, includes a linear park above with commercial stores below. The park's extraordinary appeal derives from its many prominent biophilic features, including the widespread use of plants, organic shapes and forms, natural materials, areas of prospect and refuge, organized complexity, and the integration of the natural and built environments.

temporary city remain real and formidable. Not all aspects of nature in urban areas are especially biophilic if they remain largely unrelated to the inherent human affinity for nature. An isolated garden or green roof can easily become little more than an expensive, high-maintenance decoration. And bringing nature into the modern city by focusing on the biological needs of species other than humans may be ecologically beneficial, but if these efforts are largely disconnected from the human inclination to affiliate with nature, they frequently will offer little lasting biophilic benefit (Figure 4.48).

THE COST OF BIOPHILIC DESIGN

A basic and heretofore unanswered question is the hypothetical cost of biophilic design. This figure, of course, will vary considerably depending on the circumstances, finances, ambitions, short- and long-term presumed payback of a project, and more. Any cost estimate, thus, is highly speculative. Still, one should assume that any significant addition of time, materials, planning, and innovation will likely result in at least a greater initial cost.

A longer-term cost-benefit calculation can also greatly alter the final design, especially when biophilic impacts on people's health, productivity, and wellbeing are included. This more thorough cost-benefit calculation has been addressed in the work of Bill Browning and colleagues at Terrapin Bright Green in their publication "The Economics of Biophilia," revealing a quite favorable return on the investment of including biophilic design principles when health and productivity benefits were included.

Still, most developers are especially sensitive to first-cost calculations when making design and construction decisions. When confronted with the choice of expending limited resources on more space and technology or applying it to biophilic design, many

Figure 4.48. The Agora Tower in Taipei, designed by Vincent Callebaut Architectures, contains a twisted facade draped in vegetation. Except for the widespread occurrence of plants, the building contains few other biophilic features and lacks an overall coherence and apparent relationship to nearby structures.

building owners and developers opt for the former, often viewing biophilic design as a low-priority luxury.

Another financial impediment is that much contemporary large-scale construction depends on financing obtained elsewhere from persons and institutions with typically little interest in the local human or natural environment. These investors are often motivated instead to obtain a quick return on investment and to discount future benefits.

Despite these considerable obstacles, positive change in calculating the costs and benefits of applying biophilic design has been slowly occurring. Major contributing factors have been an increasingly enlightened clientele and consumers concerned with the health, productivity, and quality of life of buildings and nearby communities. Today many designers look for opportunities to offer both low environmental impact and elements of biophilic design in a combined effort called "restorative environmental design." Where these needs converge, the result is both minimal adverse impacts on natural systems and processes and an affirmative and beneficial connection to nature. This approach has immense value; see, for example, the recent renovation of the energy and materials system of Branford College, Yale University, which won an award from the U.S. Green Building Council.

So, what is the cost of biophilic design? Given these various issues, a very rough guess at the added cost is a highly subjective 10 percent. But careful and efficient planning, as well as a more precise calculation of the long-term financial, health, and productivity benefits of a biophilic designed project, can theoretically further reduce this premium.

LESSONS LEARNED

We are still striving for the ideal occurrence of biophilic design, and inevitably the innovativeness of this practice means that all human constructions can, in the end, be only a shadow of their lofty aspirations. Nonetheless, the examples provided in this book clearly offer insights into the successful application of biophilic design under certain conditions and circumstances. In particular, ten lessons emerge from this review of applied biophilic design, many relating to the principles described in Chapter 2. A number of these lessons overlap, and their order of presentation does not indicate any specific order of importance.

1. Effective biophilic designs evoke a variety of responses based on inherent values found in nature.

Many significant occurrences of biophilic design connect to people on varying levels of their inherent inclination to value nature. For example, beloved buildings like Notre Dame Cathedral, Fallingwater, or the Sydney Opera House elicit people's attention and loyalty by including elements that evoke feelings of aesthetic attraction, emotional attachment, intellectual curiosity, practical utility, environmental control, symbolic meaning, and reverential significance. The occurrence of a multiplicity of biophilic values transforms these structures from mere inanimate objects to something lifelike and has an enduring appeal for users and visitors alike.

2. Emotional attachment is key.

Effective biophilic design generates strong feelings of emotional affection and attachment. The construction of a significant building or landscape is, of course, an extraordinary intellectual and technical achievement. Yet the ultimate success of biophilic design depends on its capacity to evoke deep and enduring feelings of connection and satisfaction. Successful biophilic design is as much an emotional as an intellectual accomplishment, and it is fundamental to people's devotion to buildings and places. Ideally this emotional attachment becomes so much a part of a structure's identity that people become motivated to maintain and retain these constructions over time.

3. Experiential engagement and immersion are necessary.

Successful biophilic design relies on recurrent experience of, and immersion in, the natural features and processes of the built environment. This active participation is necessary for people to achieve the full range of physical and mental benefits of biophilic design. A structure whose appeal is transient and fleeting can exert little long-term influence on an individual or a community. Engagement requires more than isolated and sporadic enjoyment and admiration. Instead, biophilic design requires repeated experience in the context of ordinary life.

4. Direct and indirect contact with nature, as well as a satisfying experience of space and place, enhance a design's biophilic appeal.

Successful biophilic design encompasses multiple levels of experience of natural features and processes, including direct and indirect exposure to nature and meaningful contact with particular spaces and places. This diversity of experience requires a wide range of biophilic design strategies instead of a single or isolated contact with natural features. To be most effective, these multiple levels of contact with nature should be connected, mutually reinforcing, and complementary. When these interrelationships and multiple levels of experience occur, the typical result is a strong feeling of affiliation with particular structures and landscapes.

5. A strong sense of attachment to place, an essential part of biophilic design, includes both physical and social dimensions.

Effective biophilic design generally results in feelings of attachment to a structure and landscape's location. This sense of place includes both physical characteristics of an area's characteristic geography and ecology, and a social dimension indicative of its culture and history. Attachment to place rarely occurs when structures appear to stand alone and apart, becoming more sculptural and decorative than personally significant. Successful biophilic design instead contributes to a larger, more meaningful physical and psychological context. These integrated constructions enrich our sense of membership in both the human and natural communities that give added purpose and value to our lives.

6. A building or landscape should be experienced as part of a functional and integrated whole.

Effective biophilic design depends on interconnected and interrelated contact with nature and other design elements of the built environment. These connections are complementary and mutually reinforcing, together yielding an overall ecological whole. People are biological animals for whom good habitat in the built environment means being able to participate in an integrated and functional ecosystem. Effective biophilic design weaves together aspects of the inherent human affinity for nature with other design elements to produce an emergent whole that is in many ways greater than the sum of its parts.

7. Successful biophilic design enhances health, productivity, and wellbeing.

Biophilic design fundamentally addresses how we evolved in natural systems—it includes natural features that long ago contributed significantly to human fitness and survival, and so still are appealing to us in our modern, built environments. Successful biophilic design satisfies a host of people's physical and mental needs in ways that enhance health, performance, and wellbeing. Rather than being a sacrifice for the benefit of nature, biophilic design is an act of profound human self-interest.

8. Effective biophilic design contributes to the ecological resilience and integrity of the natural environment over time.

Large-scale human development inevitably causes some degree of environmental disturbance in the short run. Effective biophilic design, however, strives to enhance the productivity, resilience, and functioning of natural systems over the long term. By expanding people's connection to the larger world that they inhabit, biophilic design fosters a sense of stewardship, respect, and responsibility for maintaining and sustaining nature. Successful biophilic design expands the feeling of membership in a community of others that includes the world beyond ourselves, of which we remain a part.

9. Ideally, biophilic design motivates people to sustain, retain, and restore their structures and places.

Effective biophilic design inspires an allegiance and commitment to buildings and landscapes that in turn motivates people to maintain and retain these structures. Sustainability is more than just minimizing pollution and other adverse environmental impacts of resource use. People become impelled to keep and restore buildings and landscapes when they become degraded. Effective biophilic design fosters this level of attachment and commitment to our built environment and places.

10. Successful biophilic design contributes to a perception
of beauty and harmony.

Effective biophilic design elicits the experience of beauty and harmony in a structure
or landscape. Biophilic structures strike us as especially lovely, alluring, and balanced. This
emotion reflects the intuitive understanding that a building or landscape is in accord with
its surroundings. These constructions, in effect, help people feel especially alive and connected with their world.

Epilogue

THE ECOLOGICAL AND ETHICAL IMPERATIVE

Successfully bringing nature into the built environment will ultimately depend on our relationship with the natural world. Until we recognize that the quality of our lives remains deeply contingent on a multiplicity of inherent connections to the world beyond ourselves, we will continue to design our buildings and landscapes in ways that are disconnected from, if not alienated from, the natural world. We need to recognize that our physical, mental, and even spiritual health and wellbeing continue to rely on our relationship to nature even in our highly constructed, technologically oriented, and increasingly urban society. When we impoverish our ties to the nonhuman environment, we inevitably compromise the quality of our existence, as well as that of many other species.

This book's focus on the built environment implies a restricted examination of architectural practice, or because of my background, another kind of environmental advocacy. Yet it is more fundamentally about human evolutionary biology, the future of our society, and how we can lead lives of satisfaction and productivity. Our evolution as a species compels us to acknowledge an inherent human inclination to affiliate with nature in ways that have contributed to our collective fitness and survival. Rather than being obsolete, mounting evidence suggests that this inclination to affiliate with nature continues to be critical to people's physical and mental health and wellness.

The natural habitat of modern life, however, has largely become the indoor built environment, where we now spend 90 percent of our time. Thus, the enormous challenge facing us today is to design our buildings, landscapes, and communities in ways that nurture our inborn affinity for the natural world. Like all species, people require a good habitat to function effectively and well. We cannot lead lives of meaning and value if we are ecologically deficient and alienated from the world around us. Relying on only our own kind for a fulfilling existence invites imperiling, inadequate, and lonely lives. For reasons of self-interest, we must maintain satisfying and mutually beneficial relationships with the nonhuman environment.

The creation of a built environment inevitably alters nature in fundamental ways. But in making such a change, we are not so different from other creatures, particularly the so-called keystone species capable of transforming their environments in the process of exploiting it. Elephants on the savannah, alligators in a wetlands, sea otters on a kelp bed, even certain invertebrates such as the starfish *Pisaster ochraceus,* greatly alter their environments while utilizing and controlling them. The question is not whether these species will transform and even initially degrade their habitats, but rather what the long-term ecological consequences of this alteration will be. Will it result in permanent environmental damage, or in time a more productive and resilient natural system that offers greater biological diversity, biogeochemical flux, hydrological regulation, pollination, decomposition, and other vital ecosystem services?

Humans are capable of drastically altering nature and even permanently damaging it through their design and development of the built environment. But, like other keystone species, we can also theoretically create ecologically more productive and aesthetically appealing habitats for ourselves and other inhabitants of the natural world. In other words, successful application of biophilic design can yield complementary and mutually beneficial connections between people and nature. This view is reflected in the remarks of the biologist and conservationist René Dubos (1980): "The relationship between humankind and nature can be one of respect and love rather than domination … The outcome … can be rich, satisfying, and lastingly successful, but only if both partners are modified by their association so as to become better adapted to each other … With our knowledge and sense of responsibility … we can create new environments that are ecologically sound, aesthetically satisfying, and economically rewarding … This process of reciprocal adaptations occurs … through minor changes in the people and their environment, but a more conscious process of design can also take place" (p. 68).

This conscious process of design can and should be part of a larger effort to forge mutually beneficial relationships between people and nature. Biophilic design provides a pathway for enriching the connections between humans and the natural world. Through its effective application, we can affirm and celebrate the extraordinary benefits we derive from nature.

The dichotomy of the natural and human-built environments can be misleading and pernicious. People remain a part of nature wherever they exist, whether in the relatively wild outdoors or inside a building. An inner-city office is as much a part of nature as an undisturbed wilderness. If people lack the capacity to function well and effectively in either environment because of a prevailing disconnect from nature, they will inevitably suffer physically and mentally. Good biophilic design acknowledges that an appropriate relationship to the natural world is a fundamental basis for a productive and satisfying existence, wherever this connection might occur.

The human need for contact with nature represents more than just a pleasant aesthetic and recreational amenity. It constitutes instead the unavoidable basis for a healthy and fulfilling existence. Nature must be more than a decorative backdrop; instead it must become a source of life, as the pioneering landscape architect Ian McHarg (1995) explained: "Clearly the problem of man and nature is not one of providing a decorative background for the human play, or even ameliorating the grim city: it is the necessity of sustaining nature as source of life, milieu, teacher, sanctum, challenge and, most of all, of rediscovering nature's corollary of the unknown in the self, the source of meaning" (p. 6). According to this view, the successful incorporation of nature into the built environment is an act of profound self-interest.

Successful biophilic design, in effect, transforms our ethical relationship to nature. It depends on the realization that a love for and connection to the dynamic, living beauty of the natural world are components of a healthy and productive human society. All our inherent values of nature reflect the self-interest of living in harmony with the nonhuman environment. A broad anthropocentric ethic can shift our relationship to the natural world from simply exploiter and admirer to partner and collaborator in creating places of health and productivity for human and nonhuman life alike. The successful practice of biophilic design contributes to this reverence and respect for nature, which has come to be recognized as an essential component of a worthy existence.

AFTERWORD

Cilla Kellert

In early November of 2011, Steve was diagnosed with multiple myeloma. He had been experiencing pain in his lower back. Next it spread to his neck. Soon he was having trouble walking. Then one morning he could barely get out of bed. After his doctor repeatedly dismissed his condition, we finally demanded better tests and got the bad news. We immediately saw numerous doctors, and Steve had a slew of tests to figure out what was up. All I knew was my world was now upside down. This disease is not curable, but it is treatable so that became our mantra—we would prolong Steve's life for as long as we could. We established a good team at Yale—an oncologist, a radiologist, and a surgeon—and began intensive treatments. After surgery and radiation, he was prescribed intensive medications—what we called his "toxic cocktail." That fall Steve cut back on his work dramatically, and we hunkered down at our house in New Haven. We found we were spending a lot of quality time with family and friends. There was some positive here—when we let friends know Steve's condition, they rallied around us, amazing us with their goodwill and support.

Every Thanksgiving, our tradition was to drive and ferry to our house on Martha's Vineyard, where many of our summer friends would join us for one last hurrah before the winter. That year Steve was too ill to travel by car, so we thought we couldn't make it—until, at the last moment, a very generous family friend called to tell us that he had chartered a private plane to fly us up and back for the day. How could we refuse?

At the Thanksgiving dinner with our close friends, Steve had this to say about his illness: "Please do not interpret what I am about to say as morbid or pessimistic. In fact, I never felt more full of life, optimistic, and determined to beat this cancer. Still, it has been said and I very much feel right now that death can make the spark of life glow ever more brightly measure for measure. It is the awareness and appreciation of one's mortality that can bestow a particular appreciation and thankfulness for the ordinary in life and the virtuous circle of love of family and friends. The silver lining of the challenge of the cancer I have so unexpectedly and suddenly come to confront is the perspective it has given me. First, it has offered me a greater than ever appreciation and thankfulness for the ordinary in life—its beauty, its quality, its vividness, its intensity, its clarity—the red of the fall maple leaves, the movement of the clouds across the sky, the connection of life with non-life, the circuit of energy that flows through and unites all matter including ourselves, the intrinsic meaning and purpose of existence, the continual process of unity and relation that governs the universe and the affairs of man. Second, the cancer has reinforced more than ever my appreciation and thankfulness of the love of family and friends, reminding me of what is most important in life, and enhancing my ability both to receive and give love. These past few weeks have been such a glorious and wonderful outpouring of love from most of all Cilla, my girls, as well as friends. This has enhanced and sharpened my appreciation of love and my capacity both to experience and express it."

Steve's illness went into remission and we had a blissful five more years together. There still were times when he was hurting and we had to try a new combination of drugs, but his zest and appreciation for life was our mainstay. He continued to write books, teach, start and complete new projects, and even go on several hunting trips. Above all, we, as a couple, continued to live life to its fullest and travel all over the globe. Steve once

Steve and Cilla on their last trip together to Lake Louise in Banff in the Canadian Rockies, September 2016.

described our union as an entity more complex than the simple sum of our separate selves, connected by faith, perseverance and love, with the result truly amazing and beautiful. One thing about Steve, he never fell short when it came to expressing himself.

In the summer of 2016, Steve started to hurt again and I was worried. I tried to get him to slow down and see his doctors. He had two bouts with pneumonia that landed him in the hospital. But he continued on: that year he had three big projects—completing a National Initiative Report to understand and connect Americans and nature (he had produced the very first one back in the 1970s under the aegis of the US Fish & Wildlife Service), serving on a Blue Ribbon Panel of top government officials and non-profit conservation organization experts examining the future of America's wildlife, and, of course, finishing this book. He was so dedicated to each project. We still managed to spend time at our favorite places—our house on the water on the Vineyard and our farm in Vermont—and we continued to travel the globe with trips to France's Côte d'Azur and the Canadian Rockies. But by the early fall, Steve's health had started to nosedive. We again tried a new regime of drugs, but this time the meds failed him. Steve lost about fifty pounds in a matter of weeks and became diabetic. His poor body finally gave up. In late November he entered hospice, where he died within twenty-four hours.

Toward the end, Steve was still working on this book, but then I took over and assisted with getting his final thoughts down on paper, numerous editing revisions, and the final production. Finishing this book for Steve has been tremendously therapeutic for me. Each time I go to it, we have our familiar conversation about his passion for biophilia.

It has been a bit sad this early spring without Steve. After his morning walks with the dogs, usually in East Rock Park, he would always come home with news of the changing season. First it would be the skunk cabbage in the wetlands near the Mill River. Then it would be the Dutchman's breeches or the crocuses that had cropped up. A variety of birds was always on the water or in the trees, and sure enough, the red winged black bird would finally sound the arrival of spring full force. The seasonal migration of the warblers was truly an exciting time for him. He would sit on our back deck with binoculars in hand ready to admire whatever yellow beauty flew into our trees. And then came the blue scilla flower, which was a personal favorite of mine. In Vermont, Steve would search for the red trillium in our nearby woods or stay awake at night listening to the spring peepers, which could be deafening. If we happened to venture to the Vineyard in early spring, he would always come home from a walk in the West Chop woods with news of sighting some rare pink lady slippers.

Steve was so observant about nature and the world around him. I had always valued nature and the outdoors, but his enthusiasm and deep awareness of our surroundings took me to a new level. Our years together of traveling around the world, with always a keen eye to the environment around us, have forever changed me.

In going through Steve's materials, I was so impressed with the voluminous articles he published on so many topics—from people's knowledge of and attitudes toward nature, to wolves, to animal cruelty, to hunters, to whales, to, of course, biophilic design. He is still getting countless views and gaining weekly achievements on ResearchGate where his work is published online. Even though his research seemingly spanned such a broad sweep of so many topics, it all revolved around a common theme—our inherent affinity to connect to nature and the outdoors.

Some of Steve's last thoughts were about biophilia and how important it is. I hope, then, that this book on biophilic design will be part of his rich legacy to the planet. I also hope to end on a happier note—recognizing that now he is at peace and at one with nature and the world. And, of course, who could forget the twinkle in his eye, his sense of joy and wonder, his great sense of humor, his intelligence yet humbleness, his love of others, and his passion for that great adventure he cherished, called life.

BIBLIOGRAPHY

Alcock, Ian, et al. 2014. "Longitudinal Effects on Mental Health of Moving to Greener and Less Green Urban Areas." *Environmental Science & Technology* 48, no. 2: 1247–1255.

Almusaed, Amjad. 2011. *Biophilic and Bioclimatic Architecture: Analytical Therapy for the Next Generation of Passive Sustainable Architecture.* London: Springer-Verlag.

Alvarsson, Jesper J., Stefan Wiens, and Mats E. Nilsson. 2010. "Stress Recovery During Exposure to Nature Sound and Environmental Noise." *International Journal Research and Public Health* 7, no. 3: 1036–1046.

Annerstedt, Matilda, and Peter Währborg. 2011. "Nature-Assisted Therapy: Systematic Review of Controlled and Observational Studies." *Scandinavian Journal of Public Health.* Pp. 1–18.

Appleton, Jay. 1996. *The Experience of Landscape.* New York: John Wiley & Sons.

Barton, Jo, and Jules Pretty. 2010. "What Is the Best Dose of Nature and Green Exercise for Improving Mental Health—A Multi-Study Analysis." *Environmental Science and Technology* 44, no. 10: 3947–3955.

Beatley, Timothy. 2011. *Biophilic Cities: Integrating Nature into Urban Design and Planning.* Washington, DC: Island Press.

Benyus, Janine. 2008. "A Good Place to Settle: Biomimicry, Biophilia, and the Return of Nature's Inspiration to Architecture." Pp. 27–42 in *Biophilic Design,* ed. Stephen R. Kellert, Judith H. Heerwagen, and Martin L. Mador. Hoboken, NJ: John Wiley & Sons.

Beute, F. Femke, and Yvonne de Kort. 2014. "Salutogenic Effects of the Environment: Review of Health Protective Effects of Nature and Daylight." *Applied Psychology: Health and Well-Being* 6, no. 1: 67–95.

Beveridge, Charles, and Paul Rocheleau. 1995. *Frederick Law Olmsted: Designing the American Landscape.* New York: Universe Books.

Bloomer, Kent C. 2000. *The Nature of Ornament: Rhythm and Metamorphosis in Architecture.* New York: Norton Books.

Bowler, Diana E., Lisette M. Buyung-Ali, Teri M. Knight, and Andrew S. Pulin. 2010. "A Systematic Review of Evidence for the Added Benefits to Health of Exposures to Natural Environments." *BioMedCentral Public Health* 10: 456–465.

Bringslimark, Tina, Grete G. Patil, and Terry Hartig. 2011. "Adaptation to Windowlessness: Do Office Workers Compensate for a Lack of Visual Access to the Outdoors?" *Environment and Behavior* 43, no. 4: 469–487.

———. "The Psychological Benefits of Indoor Plants." *Journal Environmental Psychology* 29, no. 4: 422–433.

Brousseau, Alfred. 1969. "Fibonacci Statistics in Conifers." *Fibonacci Quarterly* 7: 525–532.

Browning, William, Chris Garvin, Catherine Ryan, Namita Kallianpurkar, Leslie Labruto, Siobhan Watson, and Travis Knop. 2012. "The Economics of Biophilia." New York: Terrapin Bright Green, www.terrapinbrightgreen.com, accessed March 30, 2017.

Browning, William, and Catherine Ryan. 2016. "A Series of Case Studies of Biophilic Design." New York: Terrapin Bright Green.

Browning, William, Catherine Ryan, and Joseph Clancy. 2014. "14 Patterns of Biophilic Design: Improving Health and Well-Being in the Built Environment." New York: Terrapin Bright Green.

Cama, Rosalyn. 2009. *Evidence-Based Healthcare Design.* Hoboken, NJ: John Wiley & Sons.

Cooper-Marcus, Claire, and Naomi A. Sachs. 2013. *Therapeutic Landscapes: An Evidence-Based Approach to Designing Healing Gardens and Restorative Outdoor Spaces.* Hoboken, NJ: John Wiley & Sons.

Cooper-Marcus, Claire, and Marni Barnes, eds. 1999. *Healing Gardens: Therapeutic Benefits and Design Recommendations.* New York: John Wiley & Sons.

Corbett, Michael, and Judy Corbett. 2000. *Designing Sustainable Communities.* Washington, DC: Island Press.

Cramer, Jennifer S., and William D. Browning. 2008. "Transforming Building Practices Through Biophilic Design." Pp. 27–42 in *Biophilic Design,* ed. Stephen R. Kellert, Judith H. Heerwagen, and Martin L. Mador. Hoboken, NJ: John Wiley & Sons.

Dosen, Annemarie S., and Michael J. Ostwald. 2014. "Prospect and Refuge Theory: Constructing a Critical Definition for Architecture and Design." *International Journal of Design in Society* 6, no. 1: 9–24.

Dubos, René. *Wooing of the Earth.* New York: Scribner, 1980.

Frame, Michael, and Amelia Urry. 2016. *Fractal Worlds: Grown, Built, and Imagined.* New Haven: Yale University Press.

Friedmann, Erika. 1983. "Animal-Human Bond: Health and Wellness." In *New Perspectives on Our Lives with Companion Animals,* ed. Aaron H. Katcher and Alan M. Beck. Philadelphia: University of Pennsylvania Press.

Frumkin, Howard. 2001. "Beyond Toxicity: Human Health and the Natural Environment." *American Journal of Preventive Medicine* 20, no. 3: 234–240.

———. 2008. "Nature Contact and Human Health: Building the Evidence Base." Pp. 107–118 in *Biophilic Design,* ed. Stephen R. Kellert, Judith H. Heerwagen, and Martin L. Mador. Hoboken, NJ: John Wiley & Sons.

Gillis, Kaitlyn, and Birgitta Gatersleben. 2015. "A Review of Psychological Literature on the Health and Wellbeing Benefits of Biophilic Design." *Buildings* 5: 948–963.

Grahn, Patrik, and Ulrika K. Stigsdotter. 2010. "The Relation Between Perceived Sensory Dimensions of Urban Green Space and Stress Restoration." *Landscape and Urban Planning* 94, nos. 3–4: 264–275.

Gray, Tonia, and Carol Birrell. 2014. "Are Biophilic-Designed Site Office Buildings Linked to Health Benefits and High Performing Occupants?" *International Journal of Environmental Research and Public Health* 11, no. 12: 12204–12222.

Hagerhall, Caroline, Terry Purcell, and Richard Taylor. 2004. "Fractal Dimension of Landscape Silhouette Outlines as a Predictor of Landscape Preference." *Journal of Environmental Psychology* 24, no. 2: 247–255.

Hartig, Terry, Tina Bringslimark, and Grete G. Patil. 2008. "Restorative Environmental Design: What, When, Where, and For Whom?" Pp. 133–151 in *Biophilic Design,* ed. Stephen R. Kellert, Judith H. Heerwagen, and Martin L. Mador. Hoboken, NJ: John Wiley & Sons.

Hartig, Terry, Marlis Mang, and Gary W. Evans. 1991. "Restorative Effects of Natural Environment Experiences." *Environment and Behavior* 23, no. 1: 3–26.

Heerwagen, Judith H. 2000. "Do Green Buildings Enhance the Well Being of Workers? Yes." *Environmental Design and Construction,* July/August.

Heerwagen, Judith H., and Bret Gregory. 2008. "Biophilia and Sensory Aesthetics." Pp. 227–241 in *Biophilic Design,* ed. Stephen R. Kellert, Judith H. Heerwagen, and Martin L. Mador. Hoboken, NJ: John Wiley & Sons.

Heerwagen, Judith H., and Betty Hase. 2001. "Building Biophilia: Connecting People to Nature in Building Design." *Environmental Design and Construction.* March–April.

Heerwagen, Judith H., and Gordon H. Orians. 1986. "Adaptations to Windowlessness." *Environment and Behavior* 18: 623–639.

Hersey, George L. 1999. *The Monumental Impulse: Architecture's Biological Roots.* Cambridge, MA: MIT Press.

Heschong, Lisa. 1979. *Thermal Delight in Architecture.* Cambridge, MA: MIT Press.

Heschong Mahone Group. 2003. "Windows and Classrooms: A Study of Student Performance and the Indoor Environment." San Francisco: Pacific Gas and Electric Company.

Hildebrand, Grant. 2008. "Biophilic Architectural Space." Pp. 263–275 in *Biophilic Design,* ed. Stephen R. Kellert, Judith H. Heerwagen, and Martin L. Mador. Hoboken, NJ: John Wiley & Sons.

———. 1999. *The Origins of Architectural Pleasure.* Berkeley: University of California Press.

———. 1999. *The Wright Space: Pattern and Meaning in Frank Lloyd Wright's Houses.* Seattle: University of Washington Press.

Hosey, Lance. 2012. *The Shape of Green: Aesthetics, Ecology, and Design.* Washington, DC: Island Press.

International Well Building Institute. 2014. "The WELL Building Standard." New York: IWBI, http://www.wellcertified.com/standard, accessed March 30, 2017.

Jones, Judy, and William Wilson. 2006. *An Incomplete Education: 3,684 Things You Should Have Learned but Probably Didn't.* New York: Ballantine.

Jones, Owen. 1986. *The Grammar of Ornament.* London: Studio Editions.

Joye, Yannick. 2007. "Architectural Lessons from Environmental Psychology: The Case of Biophilic Architecture." *Review of General Psychology* 11, no. 4: 305–328.

Joye, Yannick, and Agnes E. van den Berg. 2012. "Restorative Environments." In *Environmental Psychology: An Introduction,* ed. Linda Steg, Agnes E. van den Berg, and Judith I. M. de Groot. Hoboken, NJ: John Wiley & Sons.

Kaplan, Rachel, and Stephen Kaplan. 1998. *The Experience of Nature: A Psychological Perspective.* Cambridge, UK: Cambridge University Press.

Kaplan, Stephen, Rachel Kaplan, and Robert Ryan. 1998. *With People in Mind: Design and Management of Everyday Life.* Washington, DC: Island Press.

Kellert, Stephen R. 2012. *Birthright: People and Nature in the Modern World.* New Haven: Yale University Press.

———. 2015. "Build Nature into Education." *Nature* 523: 288–289.

———. 2005. *Building for Life: Understanding and Designing the Human-Nature Connection.* Washington, DC: Island Press.

———. 2008. "Dimensions, Elements, and Attributes of Biophilic Design." Pp. 3–19 in *Biophilic Design,* ed. Stephen R. Kellert, Judith H. Heerwagen, and Martin L. Mador. Hoboken, NJ: John Wiley & Sons.

———. 1997. *Kinship to Mastery: Biophilia in Human Evolution and Development.* Washington, DC: Island Press.

Kellert, Stephen R., and David J. Case & Associates. 2016. "Preliminary Results of a National Study of Children and Nature." New Haven: Yale University School of Forestry and Environmental Studies.

Kellert, Stephen R., and Bill Finnegan. 2011. "Biophilic Design: The Architecture of Life." Sixty-minute video available at www.bullfrogfilms.com, accessed March 30, 2017.

Kellert, Stephen R., and Judith H. Heerwagen. 2007. "Nature and Healing: The Science, Theory, and Promise of Biophilic Design." In Robin Guenther and Gail Vittori, eds., *Sustainable Healthcare Architecture.* Hoboken, NJ: John Wiley.

Kellert, Stephen R., Judith H. Heerwagen, and Martin L. Mador, eds. 2008. *Biophilic Design: The Theory, Science, and Practice of Bringing Buildings to Life.* Hoboken, NJ: John Wiley & Sons.

Kellert, Stephen R., and Edward O. Wilson, eds. 1993. *The Biophilia Hypothesis.* Washington, DC: Island Press.

Küller, Rikard, and Carin Lindsten. 1992. "Health and Behavior of Children in Classrooms with and Without Windows." *Journal of Environmental Psychology* 12, no. 4: 305–317.

Kuo, Frances E. 2010. "Parks and Other Green Environments: Essential Components of a Healthy Human Habitat." Washington, DC: National Recreation and Park Association.

Kuo, Frances E., and Andrea F. Taylor. 2004. "A Potential Natural Treatment for Attention-Deficit/Hyperactive Disorder: Evidence from a National Study." *American Journal of Public Health* 94, no. 9: 1580–1586.

Larsen, Larissa, Jeffrey Adams, Brian Deal, and Elizabeth Tyler. 1998. "Plants in the Workplace: The Effects of Plant Density on Productivity, Attitudes, and Perceptions." *Environment and Behavior* 30, no. 3: 261–281.

Lawrence, Elizabeth A. 1993. "The Sacred Bee, the Filthy Pig, and the Bat out of Hell: Animal Symbolism as Cognitive Biophilia." Pp. 301–341 in *The Biophilia Hypothesis,* ed. Stephen R. Kellert and Edward O. Wilson. Washington, DC: Island Press.

Leather, Phil, Mike Pyrgas, Di Beale, and Claire Lawrence. 1998. "Windows in the Workplace: Sunlight, View, and Occupational Stress." *Environment and Behavior* 30, no. 6: 739–762.

Le Carré, John. 2015. *Our Game.* New York: Random House.

Li, Qing. 2010. "Effect of Forest Bathing Trips on Human Immune Function." *Environmental Health and Preventive Medicine* 15, no. 1: 9–17.

Lichtenfeld, Stephanie, Andrew J. Elliot, Markus A. Maier, and Reinhard Pekrun. 2012. "Fertile Green: Green Facilitates Creative Performance." *Personality and Social Psychology Bulletin* 38, no. 6: 784–797.

Living Building Challenge 3.0. 2014. "Biophilic Environment," section 9. International Living Future Institute. Seattle. https://living-future.org.

Lottrup, Lene, Patrik Grahn, and Ulrika K. Stigsdotter. 2013. "Workplace Greenery and Perceived Level of Stress: Benefits of Access to a Green Outdoor Environment at the Workplace." *Landscape and Urban Planning* 110: 5–11.

Louv, Richard. 2011. *The Nature Principle.* Chapel Hill, NC: Algonquin Books.

Mador, Martin L. 2008. "Water, Biophilic Design, and the Built Environment." Pp. 43–57 in *Biophilic Design,* ed. Stephen R. Kellert, Judith H.

Heerwagen, and Martin L. Mador. Hoboken, NJ: John Wiley & Sons.

Mandelbrot, Benoit. 1983. *The Fractal Geometry of Nature.* San Francisco: W.W. Freeman.

McHarg, Ian L. 1995. *Design with Nature.* New York: John Wiley & Sons.

Mead, M. Nathaniel. 2008. "Benefits of Sunlight." *Environmental Health Perspectives* 116, no. 4: 160–167.

Mehaffy, Michael W., and Nikos A. Salingaros. 2015. *Design for a Living Planet: Settlement, Science, and the Human Future.* Portland, OR: Sustasis Press.

Moore, Robin, and Clare C. Marcus. 2008. "Healthy Planet, Healthy Children: Designing Nature into the Daily Spaces of Childhood." Pp. 153–203 in *Biophilic Design,* ed. Stephen R. Kellert, Judith H. Heerwagen, and Martin L. Mador. Hoboken, NJ: John Wiley & Sons.

Nicklas, Michael H., and Gary B. Bailey. 1995. "Student Performance in Daylit Schools." *Innovative Design,* http://www.innovativedesign.net/Profile-Resources-Technical-Papers.html, accessed March 30, 2017.

Nute, Kevin. 2004. *Vital: Using Weather to Bring Buildings and Sustainability to Life.* Apple iBook Store.

Nyrud, Anders Q., Tina Bringslimark, and Kristian Bysheim. 2013. "Benefits from Wood Interior in a Hospital Room: A Preference Study." *Architectural Science Review* 57: 125–131.

Öhman, Arne. 1986. "Face the Beast and Fear the Face: Animal and Social Fears as Prototypes for Evolutionary Analyses of Emotion." *Psychophysiology* 23.

Orians, Gordon H. 2014. *Snakes, Sunrises, and Shakespeare: How Evolution Shapes Our Loves and Fears.* Chicago: University of Chicago Press.

Park, Bum-Jin, Yuko Tsunetsugu, Tamami Kasetani, Takeshi Morikawa, Takahide Kagawa, and Yoshifumi Miyazaki. 2009. "Physiological Effects of Forest Recreation in a Young Conifer Forest in Hinokage Town, Japan." *Silva Fennica* 43, no. 2: 291–301.

Peck, Steven W., ed. 2012. *The Rise of Living Architecture.* Toronto: Green Roofs for Healthy Cities.

Pretty, Jules, and David Pencheon. 2016. "The Seven Heresies of Asclepius: How Environmental and Social Context Shape Health and Well-Being. In *Green Exercise: Linking Nature, Health and Well-Being,* ed. Jo Barton, Rachel Bragg, and Carly Wood. London: Routledge.

Qin, Jun, Xin Zhou, H. Leng, and Z. Lian. 2014. "The Effect of Indoor Plants on Human Comfort." *Indoor Building Environment* 23: 709–723.

Ramzy, Nelly. 2015. "Biophilic Qualities in Historic Architecture." *Sustainable Cities Society* 15: 42–56.

Ratcliffe, Eleanor, Birgitta Gatersleben, and Paul T. Sowden. 2013. "Bird Sounds and Their Contributions to Perceived Attention Restoration and Stress Recovery." *Journal of Environmental Psychology* 36: 221–228.

Relph, Edward. 1976. *Place and Placelessness.* London: Pion.

Ryan, Catherine O., William D. Browning, Joseph O. Clancy, Scott L. Andrews, and Namita B. Kallianpurkar. 2014. "Biophilic Design Patterns: Emerging Nature-Based Parameters for Health and Wellbeing in the Built Environment." *Arch-net International Journal of Architectural Research* 8, no. 2: 62–76.

Salingaros, Nikos A. 2015. *Biophilia and Healing Environments.* New York: Terrapin Bright Green.

Salingaros, Nikos A., and Kenneth G. Madsen II. 2008. "Neuroscience, the Natural Environment, and Building Design." Pp. 59–83 in *Biophilic Design,* ed. Stephen R. Kellert, Judith H. Heerwagen, and Martin L. Mador. Hoboken, NJ: John Wiley & Sons.

Selhub, Eva M., and Alan C. Logan. 2012. *Your Brain on Nature: The Science of Nature's Influence on Your Health, Happiness, and Vitality.* Mississauga, ON: John Wiley & Sons.

Shibata, Seiji, and Naoto Suzuki. 2004. "Effects of an Indoor Plant on Creative Task Performance and Mood." *Scandinavian Journal of Psychology* 45: 373–381.

Stamps, Arthur. 2008. "Some Findings on Prospect and Refuge." *Perceptual and Motor Skills* 107: 141–158.

Sternberg, Esther M. *Healing Spaces: The Science of Place and Well-Being.* Cambridge, MA: Belknap Press, 2009.

Sullivan, William C., and Frances E. Kuo. 1996. "Do Trees Strengthen Urban Communities, Reduce Domestic Violence?" USDA Forest Service, Southern Region, Urban and Community Forestry Assistance Program, Athens, GA, vol. 56.

Sussman, Ann, and Justin B. Hollander. 2015. *Cognitive Architecture: Designing for How We Respond to the Built Environment.* New York: Routledge.

Taylor, Andrea F., Frances E. Kuo, and William C. Sullivan. 2001. "Coping with ADD: The Surprising Connection to Green Places." *Environment and Behavior* 33, no. 1: 55–71.

Townsend, Mardie, and Rona Weerasuriya. 2010. "Beyond Blue to Green: The Benefits of Contact with Nature for Mental Health and Wellbeing," https://www.beyondblue.org.au, accessed March 30, 2017.

Tsunetsugu, Yuko, Yoshifumi Miyazaki, and Hiroshi Sato. 2007. "Physiological Effects in Humans Induced by the Visual Stimulation of Room Interiors with Different Wood Quantities." *Journal of Wood Science* 53, no. 11: 11–16.

Ulrich, Roger S. 1993. "Biophilia, Biophobia, and Natural Landscapes." Pp. 73–137 in *The Biophilia Hypothesis,* ed. Stephen R. Kellert and Edward O. Wilson. Washington, DC: Island Press.

———. 2008. "Biophilic Theory and Research for Healthcare Design." Pp. 87–106 in *Biophilic Design,* ed. Stephen R. Kellert, Judith H. Heerwagen, and Martin L. Mador. Hoboken, NJ: John Wiley & Sons.

Ulrich, Roger S., et al. 1991. "Stress Recovery During Exposure to Natural and Urban Environments." *Journal of Environmental Psychology* 11, no. 3: 201–230.

———. 1984. "View Through a Window May Influence Recovery." *Science* 224, no. 2: 420–421.

Van den Berg, Anges. 2012. "Health Benefits of Nature." Pp. 47–56 in *Environmental Psychology: An Introduction,* ed. Linda Steg, Agnes E. van den Berg, and Judith I. M. de Groot. Hoboken, NJ: John Wiley & Sons.

Van den Berg, Anges, Terry Hartig, and Henk Statts.

2007. "Preference for Nature in Urbanized Societies: Stress, Restoration, and the Pursuit of Sustainability." *Journal of Social Issues* 63: 79–96.

Wells, Nancy M., and Kimberly Rollings. 2012. "The Natural Environment: Influences on Human Health and Function." In *The Oxford Handbook of Environmental and Conservation Psychology,* ed. Susan Clayton. London: Oxford University Press.

White, Emma, and Birgitta Gatersleben. 2011. "Green on Residential Buildings: Does It Affect Preferences and Perceptions of Beauty?" *Journal of Environmental Psychology* 31: 89–98.

White, Matthew, et al. 2010. "Blue Space: The Importance of Water for Preference, Affect, and Restorativeness Ratings of Natural and Built Scenes." *Journal of Environmental Psychology* 30: 482–493.

Wilson, Edward O. 1984. *Biophilia: The Human Bond with Other Species.* Cambridge, MA: Harvard University Press.

———. 2008. "A Conversation with E. O. Wilson." *Nova,* April 1. Available at http://www.pbs.org /wgbh/nova/nature/conversation-eo-wilson .html, accessed March 30, 2017.

Windhager, Sonja, Klaus Atzwanger, Fred L. Bookstein, and Katrin Schaefer. 2011. "Fish in a Small Aquarium—An Ethological Investigation of Biophilia." *Landscape and Urban Planning* 99, no. 1: 23–30.

Wolf, Kathleen L. 2015. Green Cities: Good Health, web database available at www.greenhealth .washington.edu, accessed March 30, 2017.

ILLUSTRATION CREDITS

Michael D. Beckwith, photo: 3.43;

Patrick Bingham-Hall, photos: 3.2, 4.12;

Patrick Bingham-Hall for Guz Architects, photo: 4.32;

Kent Bloomer Studio photograph, photo: 3.20;

Paula Borowska, photo: 3.28;

Artist: Gordon Carlisle, Eliot, ME, mural triptych for Exeter Hospital, Exeter, NH, 1995, photo: 4.15;

Cobble Hill Puzzle Company Copyright 2011, photo: 4.45;

Judith Corbett, photo: 4.36;

John D. Cramer, HPRES-ist blog, photo: 4.44;

Mikael Damkier/Shutterstock.com, photo: 4.41;

Richard Davies, photo: frontispiece, 3.16;

directphoto.bz/Alamy, photo: 3.9;

Courtesy of Daniele Domenicali, Photographer, photo: 4.11;

EDSA, INC., photo: 4.37;

Elnur/Shutterstock.com, photo: 4.7;

Flickr.com/xlibber, photo: 3.47;

Photos courtesy of Fregate Island Private, Oetker Collection, photos: 3.12, 3.13;

Photography © Anton Grassl, photo: 3.1;

Kodiak Greenwood, courtesy of Passport Resorts LLC, photo: 3.14;

Stephen Harrington, illustrations: 1.1, 3.19, 3.21, 3.34, 3.53;

Hemis/Alamy, photo: 4.47;

Photography by Carol M. Highsmith, Library of Congress, Prints & Photograph Division, LC-DIG-highsm-15571: photo: 4.5;

Steven Hyatt, www.thechurchesoftheworld.com, photo: 3.35;

iStock.com/andresimiging, photo: 3.29;

iStock.com/lifehouseimage, photo: 3.18;

iStock.com/Meinzahn, photo: 3.37;

iStock.com/TonyV3112, photo: 3.40;

iStock.com/victormaschek, photo: 3.30;

Christopher Frederick Jones, photo: 3.52;

Courtesy of Rev. Taka Kawakami, Shunkoin-Temple, Kyoto, photo: 4.1;

Stephen R. Kellert, photos: 3.6, 3.7, 3.15, 3.17, 3.22, 3.23, 3.24, 3.25, 3.27, 3.31, 3.36, 3.39, 3.44, 3.45, 3.51, 4.2, 4.9, 4.19, 4.20, 4.21, 4.22, 4.23, 4.24, 4.26, 4.28, 4.38, 4.40;

Martine Hamilton Knight, © Martine Hamilton Knight Photography, photo, 3.3;

Photo by Andrés García Lachner; designed by Benjamin García Saxe Architecture, photo: 3.49;

Emily Lerner, photo in Afterword;

INDEX

Note: Page numbers in italics indicate photographs.